Merton's witness for peace is more urgent than ever in a ...
becoming rapidly more insane and feverishly impatient. His analysis of the cost of war not only to lives but to minds and imaginations, to the integrity of whole societies, is still unsurpassed. In this vivid and compelling book, Jim Forest—who has already contributed so much to our understanding of Merton—weaves together a comprehensive reading of Merton's own thinking with personal testimony and reflection. A book of enormous richness and serious challenge.

—**Rowan Williams**

A master peacemaker's masterpiece, here is one of the best tributes honoring Merton as a contemplative peacemaker, written by someone who is himself a faithful "living text" on nonviolence. Here is a call to action, an invitation for us to live and love our humankind beyond despair.

—**Jonathan Montaldo,** editor,
We Are Already One: Thomas Merton's Message of Hope

When Dorothy Day handed her young co-worker Jim Forest a letter from Thomas Merton and asked him to answer it, a transforming journey began. The monk and the activist bonded in a profound correspondence and friendship. Its latest fruit is Jim's beautiful exploration of his friend Tom's passion for peacemaking and the abolition of war before it abolishes us. Forest goes to the heart of Merton's understanding of our fearful predicament. May we have the courage to go with them into the light.

—**Jim Douglass**, author,
JFK and the Unspeakable

This wise and hopeful book calls each of us to undertake the apostolic work of patiently pursuing, praying, and sacrificing for peace by directing us to live in communion with the Truth—the perfect love who is our peace, Jesus Christ.

— **Shawn T. Storer**, director,
Catholic Peace Fellowship

Writing from the vantage point of a lifetime dedicated to working for peace, Jim Forest explores the heart of Merton's thought and writing on issues of war, peace, and nonviolence. Forest's reflections on Merton's "advice to peacemakers" pierce to the core of Merton's thinking and are as timely now in the twenty-first century as they were in Merton's lifetime.

—**Paul M. Pearson,** director,
Thomas Merton Center

Jim Forest has written a stunning work focused on Thomas Merton as a pastor to peacemakers. Written in an inviting style, carefully researched, and rich in insight, thanks to Forest's friendship with Merton, this book introduces a new generation to Merton's legacy as one of American Catholicism's most dynamic advocates of nonviolence in the nuclear era. *The Root of War Is Fear* is destined to become a classic study of Merton's contribution to American Catholic social and religious thought.

—**Anne Klejment**,
University of St. Thomas

Jim Forest's lucid account of Merton's advice to social activists half a century ago illuminates how relevant the monk's ideas are to our time. Forest's own long engagement in the struggle for justice and peace, as well as his close friendship with Merton, makes him the ideal chronicler of this important aspect of Merton's thought.

—**Bonnie Thurston,** former president,
The International Thomas Merton Society

The Root of War Is Fear

The Root of War Is Fear

THOMAS MERTON'S ADVICE TO PEACEMAKERS

by

Jim Forest

ORBIS BOOKS
Maryknoll, New York

ORBIS BOOKS
Maryknoll, New York 10545

Fathers and Brothers
MARYKNOLL
TOGETHER IN GOD'S MISSION OF MERCY

Founded in 1970, Orbis Books endeavors to publish works that enlighten the mind, nourish the spirit, and challenge the conscience. The publishing arm of the Maryknoll Fathers and Brothers, Orbis seeks to explore the global dimensions of the Christian faith and mission, to invite dialogue with diverse cultures and religious traditions, and to serve the cause of reconciliation and peace. The books published reflect the views of their authors and do not represent the official position of the Maryknoll Society. To learn more about Maryknoll and Orbis Books, please visit our website at www.maryknollsociety.org.

Study Guide: To assist groups reading this book, the Catholic Peace Fellowship has prepared a study guide: http://catholicpeacefellowship.org/wp/wordpress/study-guide-for-the-root-of-war/

Queries regarding rights and permissions should be addressed to: Orbis Books, P.O. Box 302, Maryknoll, New York 10545-0302.

Manufactured in the United States of America.

Library of Congress Cataloging-in-Publication Data

Names: Forest, Jim (James H.), author.
Title: The root of war is fear : Thomas Merton's advice to peacemakers / Jim Forest.
Description: Maryknoll : Orbis Books, 2016. | Includes bibliographical references and index.
Identifiers: LCCN 2016002601 (print) | LCCN 2016015107 (ebook) | ISBN 9781626981973 (pbk.) | ISBN 9781608336579 (ebook)
Subjects: LCSH: Merton, Thomas, 1915-1968. | Merton, Thomas, 1915-1968—Correspondence. | Peace—Religious aspects—Christianity. | Nonviolence—Religious aspects—Christianity. | Forest, Jim (James H.)—Correspondence.
Classification: LCC BX4705.M542 F667 2016 (print) | LCC BX4705.M542 (ebook) |
DDC 271/.12502—dc23
LC record available at https://lccn.loc.gov/2016002601

For
Robert Ellsberg and Tom Cornell
and
Harry and Lyn Isbell

There is one winner, only one winner, in war.
The winner is war itself.
Not truth, not justice, not liberty, not morality.
*These are the vanquished.**

— Thomas Merton

---

* From "Target Equals City," an essay I received from Merton on February 6, 1962. It came with the note, "I consider this important—[but] publication was not permitted by censors of the Order. TM" The text, published only after Merton's death, is among those collected in *Passion for Peace* (PFP), 27-36.

Contents

A Note to Readers

The Cistercian monk Thomas Merton remains a source of spiritual inspiration and a guide for many people. Merton was above all a man of prayer, a thinker who challenged the certitudes of his time and opened new horizons for souls and for the Church. He was also a man of dialogue, a promoter of peace between peoples and religions.

— Pope Francis

Just as I was finishing this book, Pope Francis, speaking before both Houses of Congress in Washington, DC, on September 24, 2015, described Thomas Merton as one of four Americans he especially admired. The other three were Abraham Lincoln, Martin Luther King, Jr., and Dorothy Day. Probably only the names of Lincoln and King were familiar to most of the pope's audience. In the hours and days that followed many newspaper articles and web postings sought to answer the question: Who was Dorothy Day? Who was Thomas Merton?

Hoping their curiosity lingers, I'd like to think some members of Congress and other puzzled people might become readers of this book.

Anyone who searches the name "Thomas Merton" will quickly discover that he was a famous convert, a man of the world who amazed his friends by entering a more-or-less medieval Trappist monastery in rural Kentucky, who wrote an autobiography that became a surprise bestseller, and helped acquaint a modern audience with the living monastic tradition as well as the practice of contemplative prayer. They will learn that through his many books he became one of the most widely read and influential spiritual writers of his time. They might also learn that in his later years he branched out beyond traditional "spiritual" themes to address the burning social issues of the day—particularly the threat of nuclear war, racial injustice, and the war in Vietnam. Many people, including members of his own religious order, were surprised or shocked by this turn, which put him far outside the mainstream of Catholic opinion at the time. During the last decade of his life his advocacy of peace, disarmament, and nonviolence made him controversial to the point of his being silenced on the topic of war by the head of his monastic order.

It was through Merton's engagement with these contentious themes that I came to know him. First through the Catholic Worker community, and then my engagement in the emerging Catholic peace movement, I engaged in frequent correspondence plus two visits with Merton during the last seven years of his life. The topics involved not only Merton's thoughts on peace and nonviolence, his own struggles within the church and his order to express his views, but also his critical eye on peace activism. Not everything done in the name of peace, for Merton, truly advanced the spirit of peace. Merton's spiritual discernment was focused not only on what he saw as the pathologies of modern ideology and power but also on the spiritual temptations and risks faced by those who, seeking peace, were struggling to build a less destructive world.

Would that the major themes that were at the core of our conversation were less relevant in the present world! Yesterday's "cold war" has evolved into today's "war on terrorism"—contrasting phrases animated with a similar idea: that because "our side" stands for freedom, democracy, reverence for life, whatever we do (torture, mass bombing, etc.) is good, while whatever our enemies do is evil.

We find ourselves in the midst of what Pope Francis has aptly described as "a piecemeal world war three." Wars are being fought and innocent blood being shed in the Middle East, large parts of Africa, areas of Asia and Latin America as well as parts of the former Soviet Union.[1] Countless innocent people, mainly the most

---

1. The Wars in the World website—www.warsintheworld.com—currently lists sixty-six wars in progress.

vulnerable members of society, die or are gravely wounded each day. The nonphysical damage of even "minor" wars also has to be considered—post-traumatic stress disorder is a dry clinical phrase for the psychological, moral, and spiritual damage suffered by countless people, whether soldiers or civilians, who have found themselves caught in the hurricane of military violence. Weapons of mass destruction stand poised for use. The possibility confronts us of war using nuclear weapons, a war of incalculable destruction that would dwarf the two world wars fought in the twentieth century, a war in which not only vast numbers of people are targeted but the planet's environment becomes a casualty of war.

While Merton's writing ended with his death in December 1968, the subtitle of this book, *Thomas Merton's Advice to Peacemakers*, is intended to stress that the guidance Merton offered social activists half a century ago remains timely. The question is how can I, drawing on Merton's advice, become a better peacemaker in today's world?

Rereading his many letters to me not only revived memories of Merton and myself as we were in the tumultuous sixties but also awoke a feeling that what Merton shared with me then could speak intimately to a new generation of those inspired to take up the struggle for peace and justice. You hold the result in your hands.

Feast of All Souls, November 2, 2015

A Word of Thanks

THIS BOOK HAD ITS ORIGINAL INSPIRATION in the months following Merton's death. I envisioned putting together a small book entitled *Thomas Merton: Letters on Peacemaking*. Regrettably the idea went unrealized. I was not only deeply immersed in efforts to end the Vietnam War but was awaiting trial with thirteen others for burning draft records in Milwaukee in September 1968. Starting in the summer of 1969, I was to enjoy a sabbatical behind bars—thirteen months in prison for my act of civil disobedience. (While *Letters on Peacemaking* died on the vine, something similar, though on a smaller scale, took shape a decade later when Gerald Twomey invited me to write a chapter on Merton's "struggle with peacemaking" as a chapter for a book he was editing, *Thomas Merton: Prophet in the Belly of a Paradox*.)

Over the years I have written extensively on Merton, including a twice-revised biography, *Living with Wisdom*. Yet the peacemaking aspect of Merton's thought continues to be so important and at the same time so little known. Two important books by Merton, *Peace in the Post-Christian Era* and *Cold War Letters*, were banned by his abbot general and were published only four decades after his death.

My heartfelt thanks to all who played a supportive role in this project, especially Robert Ellsberg, friend, editor, publisher, and fellow hagiographer; Tom Cornell, brother in everything but DNA; Harry and Lyn Isbell, who have been in the shadows of every book I've written; Paul Pearson and Mark Meade at the Thomas Merton Center at Bellarmine University in Louisville, who time and again found what I couldn't find; Phil Runkel, responsible for the Dorothy Day/Catholic Worker archive at Marquette University in Milwaukee; Joseph Smith, assistant at the University of Notre Dame Archives; Shawn Storer and Leah Coming of the Catholic Peace

Fellowship staff; Tim Schilling for pointing out areas of the draft text that needed development; Patrick O'Connell, co-author of the ever-helpful *Thomas Merton Encyclopedia*, for many suggestions plus insightful guidance; historian Julie Leininger Pycior for her careful reading of the manuscript; the late Msgr. William Shannon, editor of *The Hidden Ground of Love* (HGL), in which many of the letters used here plus hundreds more to other correspondents can be found; and my wife, Nancy, partner, best friend, thoughtful reader, attentive editor, and major source of encouragement.

Merton writing (Photo by Jim Forest)

Jonas in the Belly of a Paradox

IN *THE SIGN OF JONAS*, Thomas Merton wrote: "Like Jonas himself I find myself traveling toward my destiny in the belly of a paradox."[1] Paradox was a word Thomas Merton appreciated, in part because there were so many paradoxes within himself. One of these was that he belonged to a religious order with a tradition of silent withdrawal and near disappearance from the world, yet through his prolific writings millions of people became familiar with his life and convictions, his temptations and inner struggles, his humor and his epiphanies. He had a talkative vocation within the silent life. From a place of intentional isolation, he was deeply—often controversially—engaged with the outside world during the last decade of his life. It was a paradox he often wished would end in favor of silence, but it never did. Like the reluctant Jonas, who sought to evade a prophet's role in saving Nineveh, Merton was delivered to the sinful city as if by whale.

As with the fabled blind men, each investigating a portion of an elephant, many people have a conception of Merton that is correct but incomplete. There are those for whom Merton is best known for his early writings, his autobiography, and his books on prayer and spirituality. Others especially appreciate his later work, for example, his exploratory essays on non-Christian religious traditions, and can be dismissive of "the early Merton." Seeing Merton whole is no small task. Certainly there was a significant evolution in Merton's writing in the late 1950s and early 1960s as he took on the responsibility of addressing the pressing social issues of his time while carving doors of dialogue in walls that divided major religious communities. Even so, for all these developments it is striking to note that a concern for

---

1. SJ, 2.

peace runs like a red thread connecting his very earliest writing and his later work.

The horrors of the First World War provided the main reference point in the opening sentences of his autobiography, *The Seven Storey Mountain* (SSM), published in 1948, when Merton, thirty-three, was seven years into monastic life:

> *On the last day of January 1915, under the sign of the Water Bearer, in a year of a great war, and down in the shadow of some French mountains on the borders of Spain, I came into the world. Free by nature, in the image of God, I was nevertheless the prisoner of my own violence and selfishness, in the image of the world into which I was born. That world was the picture of Hell, full of men like myself, loving God and yet hating Him; born to love Him, living instead in fear and hopeless self-contradictory hungers. Not many hundreds of miles away from the house where I was born, they were picking up the men who rotted in rainy ditches among the dead horses . . . in a forest without branches along the river Marne.*[2]

Among the microcosmic consequences of that Great War was its impact on the Merton family. It tore their hopes and plans to shreds. Owen and Ruth Merton were expatriate artists who had met in Paris and, after their marriage, made their home in Prades, a town in the French Pyrenees. Though a New Zealander, Owen Merton would have been subject to French military conscription had he remained in France. Owen's moral objections to war were of no consequence to the French authorities—no exceptions were made for foreigners or conscientious objectors. In the summer of 1916, Owen, Ruth, and their year-old son, Tom, left France for the United States, settling not far from Ruth's parents in Douglaston, Long Island.

Owen arrived in an America that still regarded the battles on the far side of the Atlantic as a strictly European event, but in April 1917 the United States declared war on Germany and the following month Congress authorized military conscription. Aliens were not exempt.

---

2. SSM, 3. Pope Francis quoted from this passage in his address to both houses of the U.S. Congress.

As required by law, Owen Merton registered for the draft on the fifth of June 1917, declaring at the time that he was both a conscientious objector and the sole support of wife and child.[3] He was never called up. Once war was declared, the vast majority of Americans, very likely including Ruth's family, came down with a severe case of war fever. The war was, after all, packaged as a holy crusade, nothing less than "the war to end all wars." Able-bodied men like Owen who opposed the war and refused to take part in it were widely regarded as cowards and shirkers.

Even a child knows that war produces dead bodies. While ordinarily death is a playground concept for children—*bang, bang, you're dead*—that was not the case for Tom Merton. In 1921, when he was six, death became something all too real when his mother died of cancer. For young Tom, death meant a gaping absence, a collapse of the most basic structures of life. Death meant abandonment. His mother had been abducted by death. A decade later came a second blow. Just two weeks before his sixteenth birthday Tom became an orphan. After having moved to England with Tom, Owen died of a brain tumor in a London hospital in January 1931. Apart from grandparents, who were an ocean away, all that was left of Tom's immediate family was a younger brother, John Paul, still living in America with Ruth's parents. Tom's guardian was a London physician.

At about the time of Owen's death, Tom Merton became an admirer of Gandhi, then visiting England, and of his nonviolent campaign against British imperial rule in India. Rarely one to be part of any majority, Tom took Gandhi's side in a formal debate at Oakham, his boarding school, arguing that India had every right to demand the end of British colonial rule. Merton's side in the debate was easily defeated, but for the rest of Merton's life he was to remain an advocate of Gandhi's form of struggle, what Gandhi called *satyagraha*: the nonviolent, life-protecting power that comes from seeking the conversion of opponents rather than their humiliation and destruction.

---

3. My thanks to Anne Klejment for discovering this information.

Thomas Merton 1933 passport photo.
(Courtesy Thomas Merton Center)

Among the formative events that added another layer of meaning to the word "death" and also brought him close to the annihilating potential of toxic ideologies occurred in the spring of 1932. Now seventeen and still a student at Oakham, Merton went for a solo holiday walk along the Rhine River. It was an excursion that happened to coincide with Hitler's campaign for the German chancellorship. One morning, while walking down a quiet country road lined with apple orchards, Merton was nearly run down by a car full of young Nazis. Tom dived into a ditch in the nick of time, the car's occupants showering him with Hitler election leaflets as they sped past. His jump injured a toe that soon became too painful for him to complete the hike as planned. Back at his school and in worsening pain, a doctor found Merton's veins were full of poisoned blood. Immediate hospitalization was needed. His brief encounter with German Nazis had nearly cost Merton his life.[4]

After Oakham, Merton did a year at Clare College, Cambridge— a time of "beer, bewilderment and sorrow," in the words of his friend

---

4. Thomas Merton, *My Argument with the Gestapo* (MAG), 5.

Bob Lax—then moved to his grandparents' home on Long Island, near Manhattan, where he matriculated at Columbia. Like any university student of his day, Merton found himself in a whirlpool of radical political movements. The Great Depression had drawn millions of people to the Left. For a brief time Merton was attracted to Communism, but quickly found Marxist political ideology a dead-end street.

Merton's search for deeper waters took a religious turn. Memories of his father's churchless Christianity must have haunted him, as well as his own encounters with ancient churches and their remarkable mosaics when he visited Rome two years after Owen's death. Before returning to England he had been moved to pray with tears in one of Rome's oldest churches, Santa Sabina. Later, as a university student in New York, he was on his way to Catholic Christianity. In November 1938, Merton was baptized at Corpus Christi Church in Manhattan. It was the most important border crossing of his adult life. From then on, every question was to be viewed in the light of Christ.

One of the saints who most inspired Merton was Francis of Assisi, whose radical witness to Christ's gospel in the thirteenth century included opposition to all killing. In a declaration that resonated for Merton, Francis once explained to his bishop why the members of his community renounced ownership of property:

> *If we held property, armed force for protection would become necessary. For property gives rise to lawsuits and to wars which in various ways destroy all love of God and of our fellowmen. Our membership, therefore, will not hold property.*[5]

Francis founded a movement not only of celibate brothers (and, with Saint Clare, of sisters) who lived in poverty, but he also created a "third order" of lay people, married and single, whose original

---

5. *Francis of Assisi—The Founder: Early Texts*, vol. 2, ed. Regis J. Armstrong et al. (Hyde Park, NY: New City Press, 2000), 41. The quotation is from "The Anonymous of Perugia," Chapter 3, and "The Legend of the Three Companions," Chapter 9. After the founder's death the no-property rule was modified, but the vow of voluntary poverty was never abandoned.

rule forbade members to possess or use any weapons of war, in effect, a vow that obliged them to be conscientious objectors. During the Fifth Crusade and at the risk of his own life, Francis himself gave an example of unarmed peacemaking, traveling to Egypt to meet with one of Christendom's chief opponents, Sultan Malik-al-Kamil.

St. Francis of Assisi

While teaching at a Franciscan college, Saint Bonaventure, in Olean, New York, Merton took vows as a lay Franciscan. Like other third-order members, Merton wore a simple scapular under his clothes as a reminder of his commitment—two chords over the shoulders attached to two small squares of brown material similar to the coarse fabric used in Franciscan robes.

Despite his strong Franciscan bent, at times even Merton felt the powerful tides that were drawing so many others to become soldiers in the war going on in Europe, including his own brother, John Paul. After seeing a film about the impact of the Blitz on London, Merton wrote in his journal:

> *For the first time in my life, I think, I momentarily wanted to be in the war. . . . Bombs are beginning to fall into my own life. . . . [The film] was propaganda, but good propaganda. . . . For the first time I imagined that maybe I belonged there, not here.*[6]

What especially brought the horror of city bombing home to him was a picture of a bombed-out London clothing shop in which, when he was sixteen, he had purchased a gray herringbone tweed suit.

The industrial impersonality of modern war horrified Merton:

---

6. *Run to the Mountain: The Journals of Thomas Merton 1939–1941* (RM), 244-45; entry dated October 27, 1940.

There is not even much hatred. If there were more hatred the thing would be healthier. But it was just filthy, this destruction.... This is just a vile combat of bombs against bricks, attempts to wipe out machines and to bury men lying in tunnels under tons of stone and rubble. It is not like a fight, it is like a disease.... [7]

Even in the placid countryside surrounding Olean, Merton saw strands of connection with war:

The valley is full of oil storage tanks, and oil is for feeding bombers, and once they are fed they have to bomb something, and they generally pick on oil tanks. Wherever you have oil tanks, or factories, or railroads or any of the comforts of home and manifestations of progress, in this century, you are sure to get bombers, sooner or later. Therefore, if I don't pretend ... to understand the war, I do know this much: that the knowledge of what is going on only makes it seem desperately important to be voluntarily poor, to get rid of all possessions this instant. [8]

Merton's inner wrestling with war found expression in a novel he wrote while teaching at Saint Bonaventure's, *The Journal of My Escape from the Nazis* (published posthumously in 1969 as *My Argument with the Gestapo*). The story followed Merton's imagined return from America to war-ravaged London. Though coming from America, Merton sees himself as a stateless person. "I have lived in too many countries," he explains, "to have a nationality." Why do you come back, he is asked. "Not to fight," he says. He admits he has come to write. "What will you write?" "I will say that ... the things I remember are destroyed, but that does not mean as much as it seems, because the destruction was already going on before, and destruction is all I remember."

Later the question is posed: But isn't the war Germany's fault? "In the sense that they began fighting it, yes." Doesn't that mean Germany is guilty? "I don't know the meaning of the word guilty, except in the sense that I am also guilty for the war, partly." But is

---

7. Ibid., 264; entry dated November 28, 1940.
8. Ibid., 231-32; entry dated June 16, 1940.

London under the Blitz

it not nations rather than persons that are guilty of war? "Nations don't exist. They can't be held responsible for anything. Nations are made up of people, and people are responsible for the things they do." In that case, he is told, Hitler is the guilty one. "He might be. Only I don't know enough about it. He might be more guilty than any other one person, but he isn't the only person guilty of the war. . . . All I know is, if anything happens to the world, it is partly because of me."

The narrator explains to an officer who is interrogating him:

You think you can identify a man by giving his date of birth and his address, his height, his eyes' color, even his fingerprints. Such information will help you put the right tag on his body if you should run across his body somewhere full of bullets, but it doesn't say anything about the man himself. Men become objects and not persons. Now you complain because there is a war, but war is the proper state for a world in which men are a series of numbered bodies. War is the state that now perfectly fits your philosophy of life: you deserve the war for believing the things you believe. In so far as I tend to believe those same things and act according to such lies, I am part of the complex of responsibilities for the war too. But if you want to identify me, ask me not where I live, or what I like to eat, or how I comb my hair, but ask me what I think I am living for, in detail, and ask me what I think is keeping me from living fully for the thing I want to live for.[9]

The question of how to respond as individuals should the United States join the war was the subject of long-running conversations Merton had with such close friends as Bob Lax and Ed Rice. For Merton it was a question that had to be answered not in terms of political or ideological theory or the accidents of national identity but in terms of being a follower of Christ, who killed no one, waved no flags, and blessed no wars. This led him to formulate a response—conscientious objection—that, for a Roman Catholic at that time, was unusual, to say the least. As he explained to his draft board in March 1941:

As a Franciscan Tertiary I am bound to follow a rule which is intended to help me imitate in every detail the lives of Christ and Saint Francis, who did not kill men, but went among the sick and the poor doing good. Christ told us we must love our enemies, and Saint Francis wrote in the Rule of the Tertiaries that they must love peace and heal all discord. I cannot conceive how killing a man with a flame thrower, a machine gun or a bomb is compatible with a life of Christian perfection along these lines....

Merton wrote of his willingness to undertake noncombatant duty under certain conditions:

[I am willing to serve so long as it involves] no part in the machinery that produces the death of men. Merely being a non-combatant member of a combatant unit is not enough.... I am willing and eager to serve in any post where the work is saving lives and helping those in

---

9. MAG, 160-61.

*suffering: ambulance work, hospital work, air raid protection work,
etc. I do not ask for any position that would necessarily be remote from
the line of fire, or "out of danger."*[10]

The same day Merton made an exultant entry in his journal
recording the relief he felt after posting his declaration to his draft
board:

*This has been a very remarkable day to have looked in the face. I don't
think of the contents of a day as "a day," ordinarily; but this one has to
be seen that way. To begin with, it is a day I have feared—it is the day
I got all of my notions together about war, and said them briefly all at
once, on a few sheets of paper, on a prepared blank and put them in
the mail for the Draft Board.*

*. . . I made out my reasons for being a partial conscientious objector,
for asking for noncombatant service, so not having to kill men made
in the image of God when it is possible to obey the law (as I must) by
serving the wounded and saving lives—or that may be a purely artifi-
cial situation: by serving the humiliation of digging latrines, which is
a far greater honor to God than killing men.*

*The thing was that I wrote these things out without trepidation,
and was amazed.*[11]

Here is how Merton described his conscientious objector stand
in *The Seven Storey Mountain*, published three years after the war
ended:

*[God] was not asking me to judge all the nations of the world, or to
elucidate all the moral and political motives behind their actions. He
was not demanding that I pass some critical decision defining the
innocence and guilt of all those concerned in the war. He was asking
me to make a choice that amounted to an act of love for His truth, His
goodness, His charity, His Gospel. . . . He was asking me to do, to the*

---

10. The typescript is in the collection of the Rare Book and Manuscripts
Room, Butler Library, Columbia University, New York.

11. RM, 316-17; entry dated March 4, 1941.

best of my knowledge, what I thought Christ would do. . . . After all,
Christ did say, "Whatsoever you have done to the least of these my
brethren, you did it to me."[12]

Conscientious objectors have always been a rare breed. In the
course of World War II, 34.5 million American men between the
ages of 18 and 44 registered for the draft. Out of these millions, only
72,354 applied for conscientious objector status. Of these, 27,000
failed to pass the physical exam and were exempted, as seemed to
have been the case for Bob Lax. Of those who were found physically
fit, 25,000 served in noncombatant roles in the military, the form
of conscientious objection for which Merton applied, thus agreeing to work for the Army Medical Corps or in anything that did not
involve actual combat. Opposed to any military role, approximately
12,000 men performed alternative service in the Civilian Public Service program. More than 6,000 men either chose not to cooperate
with the draft outright or failed to gain recognition as conscientious
objectors and went to prison.[13]

To appreciate how exceptional Merton's choice of conscientious
objection was, one must bear in mind that, right up to the period of
John F. Kennedy's election as president twenty years later, the patrio-
tism of American Catholics was regarded as suspect by the Protestant
majority. Catholics bent over backward to make clear their gratitude
for having found a home in America. One would find the slogan
Pro Deo et Patria—For God and Country—over the doors of many
Catholic schools. Catholics were outshining their neighbors in doing
whatever was required to be recognized as "good Americans." Merton, however, wasn't thinking of social acclimation and acceptance or
even of being seen as "a good Catholic." Rather, he was trying to make
choices that resembled those he believed Christ would make.

In 1941 Merton found himself at a vocational crossroads. One
possibility was to become a full-time staff member of Friendship

---

12. SSM, 311-12.

13. https://en.wikipedia.org/wiki/Conscientious_objector.

House, a Catholic Worker–like house of hospitality in Harlem at which he had been volunteering. This would mean a life centered in the works of mercy: feeding the hungry, giving drink to the thirsty, clothing the naked, housing the homeless, caring for the sick and the imprisoned. The other was to become part of the monastic community of a Trappist abbey, Our Lady of Gethsemani, in Kentucky, which he had visited that spring and which impressed him so profoundly that in a journal entry he described Gethsemani as the true "center of America."[14]

A secondary attraction of a monastic vocation was that, as a monk, he would automatically be exempted from military service. His draft status had just been changed—despite too many extracted teeth, he was no longer classified as physically unfit. Nor could he reasonably expect that any draft board would be willing to recognize a Catholic as a conscientious objector, a stand that was at the time mainly associated with several small Protestant "peace churches" such as the Quakers and the Mennonites.

On December 10, 1941, just three days after the Japanese attack on Pearl Harbor as it happened, Merton rang the bell of the monastery's gatehouse door over which was written the Latin words *Pax Intrantibus*—peace to all who enter. He was embracing a life that, in its totality, was an act of conscientious objection not just to war but to a war-driven world.

Once he was within the relatively unworldly enclosure of monastic life and out of harm's way, one might have thought Merton's interest in the issue of war would fade, even vanish. Not so. The hellishness of war was a topic in a number of the poems he wrote as a young monk, beginning with those collected in his first book, *Thirty Poems*, published by New Directions in 1944; and it remained a major topic in *A Man in the Divided Sea* (1946), *Figures for an Apocalypse* (1947) and *Tears of the Blind Lions* (1949).[15]

---

14. RM, 333; journal entry dated April 7, 1941.

15. See Patrick O'Connell's essay, "Landscape of Disaster: The War Poems of Thomas Merton," in the 2006 edition of *The Merton Annual*.

Entrance to the Abbey of Gethsemani under the motto,
"Pax to all who enter." (Courtesy Thomas Merton Center)

Writing his autobiography, *The Seven Storey Mountain*, a project begun in 1944 at the request of his first abbot, Dom Frederick
Dunne, what Merton had to say about conscientious objection was
not at all what readers, especially Catholics, were used to hearing.

Just before the epilogue, the book included a poem, "To My
Brother, Missing in Action," written after John Paul Merton—his
plane shot down—became a casualty of war in April 1943. One of
Merton's finest works, it is not only an expression of grief for his slain
brother but a cry of anguish for all who inhabit the cruel world of
battlefields:

> *Sweet brother, if I do not sleep*
> *My eyes are flowers for your tomb;*
> *And if I cannot eat my bread,*

My fasts shall live like willows where you died.
If in the heat I find no water for my thirst,
My thirst shall turn to springs for you, poor traveller.

Where, in what desolate and smokey country,
Lies your poor body, lost and dead?
And in what landscape of disaster
Has your unhappy spirit lost its road?

Come, in my labor find a resting place
And in my sorrows lay your head,
Or rather take my life and blood
And buy yourself a better bed—
Or take my breath and take my death
And buy yourself a better rest.

When all the men of war are shot
And flags have fallen into dust
Your cross and mine shall tell men still
Christ died on each, for both of us.

For in the wreckage of your April Christ lies slain,
And Christ weeps in the ruins of my spring:
The money of Whose tears shall fall
Into your weak and friendless hand,
And buy you back to your own land:
The silence of Whose tears shall fall
Like bells upon your alien tomb.
Hear them and come: they call you home.[16]

Mother dead, father dead, now his only brother killed in war. . . . Merton was like the Ishmael of *Moby Dick*, a sole survivor.

Perhaps it was John Paul's death in war that amplified the issue of war in Merton's thoughts, even during the years when he regarded monks as people who had divorced themselves from the world and its self-inflicted wounds.

---

16. SSM, 404.

Thomas Merton in 1949.
(Courtesy of Abbey of Gethesemani)

Reminders of war frequently entered the monastic enclosure. The noise and vibrations of artillery practice at nearby Fort Knox literally shook the hills of Gethsemani. In his poem "The Guns of Fort Knox" Merton meditated on

> *Explosions in my feet, through boards*
> *Wars work under the floor. Wars*
> *Dance in the foundations.*

The poem concludes:

> *Guns, I say, this is not*
> *The right resurrection. All day long*
> *You punch the doors of death to wake*

> A slain generation. Let them lie
> Still. Let them sleep on,
> O Guns. Shake no more
> (But leave the locks secure)
> Hell's door.[17]

Hell's door was being made all the wider by the development of weapons of mass destruction, especially the hydrogen bomb, yet many people failed to see hell's door for what it was. As Merton wrote to the philosopher Erich Fromm in 1955:

> *I feel that the blindness of men to the terrifying issue [of nuclear war] we have to face is one of the most discouraging possible signs for the future.... Fear has driven people so far into the confusion of mass-thinking that they no longer see anything except in a kind of dim dream. What a population of zombies we are! What can be expected of us?*
>
> *It seems to me that the human race as a whole is on the verge of a crime that will be second to no other except the crucifixion of Christ and it will, if it happens, be very much the same crime all over again. And then, as now, religious people are involved on the guilty side. What we are about to do is "destroy" God over again in His image, the human race.... Any person who pretends to love God in this day, and has lost his sense of the value of humanity, has also lost his sense of God without knowing it. I believe that we are facing the consequences of several centuries of more and more abstract thinking, more and more unreality in our grasp of values. We have reached such a condition that now we are unable to appreciate the meaning of being alive, of being able to think, to make decisions, to love.*[18]

Little by little the world, its beauty and its troubles reshaped Merton's spiritual life. In his journals Merton records several intense experiences of God opening his eyes in a life-changing way. One of

---

17. *The Strange Islands* (SI), 21.

18. HGL,311; letter dated March 13, 1955.

the most significant happened on March 18, 1958. On an errand that brought him to Louisville, Merton was standing at a busy downtown intersection waiting for the light to change:

In Louisville, at the corner of Fourth and Walnut, in the center of the shopping district, I was suddenly overwhelmed by the realization that I loved all those people, that they were mine and I theirs, that we could not be alien to one another even though we were total strangers. It was like waking from a dream of separateness, of spurious self-isolation in a special world, the world of renunciation and supposed holiness. The whole illusion of a separate holy existence is a dream.... This sense of liberation from an illusory difference was such a relief and such a joy to me that I almost laughed out loud.... It is a glorious destiny to be a member of the human race, though it is a race dedicated to many absurdities and one which makes many terrible mistakes: yet, with all that, God Himself gloried in becoming a member of the human race. A member of the human race! To think that such a commonplace realization should suddenly

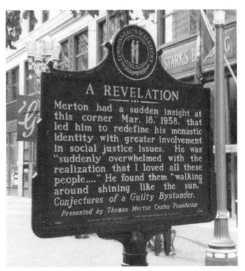

A sign commemorates Merton's epiphany on "the corner of Fourth and Walnut" in downtown Louisville.

seem like news that one holds the winning ticket in a cosmic sweep-stake. . . . There is no way of telling people that they are all walking around shining like the sun. . . . There are no strangers. . . . If only we could see each other [as we really are] all the time. There would be no more war, no more hatred, no more cruelty, no more greed. . . . I suppose the big problem is that we would fall down and worship each other. . . . [T]he gate of heaven is everywhere.[19]

This awakening marked the opening of a greater compassion within Merton. The consequences became obvious in the years that followed.

One aspect of the deeper sense of connection with the world and its people was a heightened consciousness of threats to life. He became increasingly aware that many American Christians, Catholics not least among them, were resigned to military catastrophe and were even advocates of a preemptive nuclear attack on Soviet Russia. "Better dead than Red" proclaimed a popular slogan of the period. Another was "The only good Red is a dead Red."

In late August 1961, Merton wrote in his journal:

I have been considering the possibility of writing a kind of statement —"where I stand," as a declaration of my position as a Christian, a writer and a priest in the present war crisis. There seems to be little I can do other than this. There is no other activity available to me. . . . If I can say something clear and positive it may be of some use to others as well as to myself. This statement would be for the Catholic Worker. *As a moral decision, I think this might possibly be a valid step toward fulfilling my obligations as a human being. . . .* [20]

---

19. *Conjectures of a Guilty Bystander* (CGB), 140-42.

20. *Turning toward the World* (TTW), 257; entry dated August 29, 1961. A few days later, responding to a letter from Ethel Kennedy, the president's sister-in-law, Merton expressed his "very strong objection to the resumption of testing nuclear weapons" (HGL, 443; letter dated September 4, 1961).

A Book in a Bus Terminal

MERTON ENTERED MY LIFE in December 1959 just after I had grad-
uated from the Navy Weather School and was on a two-week leave
before reporting for work with a Navy unit at the headquarters of the
U.S. Weather Service near Washington, DC. Waiting at New York's
Port Authority Bus Terminal, I noticed a carousel full of paperbacks
at a newsstand and came upon a book with an odd title, *The Seven
Storey Mountain*. The author's name, Thomas Merton, meant nothing
to me. It was, the jacket announced, "the autobiography of a young
man who led a full and worldly life and then, at the age of 26, entered
a Trappist monastery." There was a quotation from Evelyn Waugh,
who said this book "may well prove to be of permanent interest in
the history of religious experience." Another writer compared it to
Saint Augustine's *Confessions*. I bought a copy.

It proved to be a can't-put-it-down book for me. In the bus going
up the Hudson Valley, I recall occasionally looking up from the text
to gaze out the window at the heavy snow that was falling that night.
Merton's story has ever since been linked in my mind with the silent
ballet of snowflakes swirling under streetlights.

In *The Seven Storey Mountain* I discovered that Merton, when he
was precisely my age, had also been on the road, in his case in Italy.
He too was on a search, while having no clear idea what it was he was
seeking. It was while in Rome that a mosaic icon in the apse behind
the altar of one of the city's most ancient churches, Saints Cosmas
and Damian, triggered in Merton an overwhelming awareness of the
presence of God and the reality of Christ. He wrote:

> For the first time in my whole life, I began to find out something
> of who this Person was that men call Christ. It was obscure, but it
> was a true knowledge of Him. But it was in Rome that my concep-

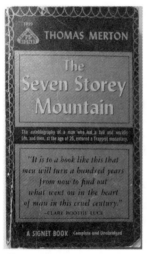

Cover of
Seven Storey Mountain

tion of Christ was formed. It was there I first saw Him, Whom I now serve as my God and my King, and who owns and rules my life. It is the Christ of the Apocalypse, the Christ of the Martyrs, the Christ of the Fathers. It is the Christ of Saint John, and of Saint Paul, and of Saint Augustine and Saint Jerome and all the Fathers, and the Desert Fathers. It is Christ God, Christ King.[1]

While Merton's religious journey was only beginning, he had been given a first glimpse of the path he was to follow.

The Seven Storey Mountain awakened in me an interest in monastic life—I saw it as a possible vocation—and incidentally also made me think more critically about war and the implications of my being in the military.

In the months that followed, I read another autobiography, Dorothy Day's *The Long Loneliness*. Here was a young writer and journalist in the thick of New York's bohemian subculture who, to the bewilderment if not horror of many leftist friends, found her way into the Catholic Church. Several years later she founded a newspaper, *The Catholic Worker*, which soon gave birth to a house of hospitality for the homeless and rapidly evolved into a widespread movement that linked the works of mercy with efforts to promote a more compassionate social order. Like Merton, Day saw war as profoundly un-Christian, a rejection of Christ's example and teaching. For Dorothy, hospitality in all its forms was at the heart of Christian life. As she wrote:

The early Christians started with the works of mercy and it was this technique which converted the world. The corporal works are to feed the hungry; to give drink to the thirsty; to clothe the naked; to harbor

---

1. SSM, 109.

the harborless; to ransom the captive; to visit the sick; to bury the dead. The spiritual works are to instruct the ignorant; to counsel the doubtful; to admonish sinners; to bear wrongs patiently; to forgive offense willingly; to comfort the afflicted; to pray for the living and the dead. Not all of these works are within the reach of all—that is understood. But that we should take part in some of them is a matter of obligation, a strict precept imposed both by the natural and Divine law.[2]

In the early fall of 1960, while still in the Navy, I began visiting the Catholic Worker at its center in lower Manhattan. It was during one of those visits that I first met and talked with Dorothy Day, who turned out to be as curious about me as I was about her. Among my surprises was the discovery that she and Merton were correspondents. I had imagined Merton was far more cut off from the outside world than was actually the case.

One letter from Merton that Dorothy shared with me soon after we met, but written by him the previous year, began with a reference to the Catholic Worker's main peace witness in those years— its annual refusal to take shelter as required by New York State Law as an exercise in civil defense. Dorothy saw such drills (conducted between 1955 and 1961) as a dress rehearsal for nuclear war with the Soviet Union. For her, civil defense was, really, a cruel joke, as subways and basements offered protection only from conventional weapons, but the ritual had the effect of making nuclear war seem survivable and even winnable. Dorothy had chosen instead to sit on a park bench in front of New York's City Hall. She had been jailed several times for her act of quiet civil disobedience, until the crowds that gathered with her became

Dorothy Day
(*Milwaukee Sentinel*)

2. Dorothy Day, *The Catholic Worker*, February 1935; www.catholicworker. org/dorothyday/articles/15.html.

Dorothy Day and others in 1955 protest the first compulsory civil defense drill in New York. (Photo: Robert Lax)

so large that the war game was abandoned. But that end was still not in sight when Merton wrote:

> *I am deeply touched by your witness for peace. You are very right in doing it along the lines of* Satyagraha *[literally "truth-force," Gandhi's word for what Western people often call nonviolence]. I see no other way, though of course the angles of the problem are not all clear. I am certainly with you on taking some kind of stand and acting accordingly. Nowadays it is no longer a question of who is right but who is at least not a criminal—if any of us can say that anymore. So don't worry about whether or not in every point you are perfectly all right according to everybody's book; you are right before God as far as you can go and you are fighting for a truth that is clear enough and important enough. What more can anybody do? . . . It was never more true that the world cannot see true values.*[3]

I don't suppose many people today can readily appreciate the significance of this and similar letters Merton was sending to Doro-

---

3. HGL, 136.

thy and others in the outside world whose work he admired. Partly thanks to Merton and Day, the Catholic peacemaker, then a rarity, was to become far more common in the years ahead and to receive support from the highest levels of the church, as we saw with Pope Francis choosing them to spotlight in his historic address to Congress. But at that time, when the Cold War might at any moment become a nuclear war, the Catholic Worker movement was viewed with considerable suspicion for its talk of "the works of mercy versus the works of war." It was tolerated because of its orthodoxy in all other respects and its direct, simple, and unpretentious commitment to the humanity of impoverished people. New York's Cardinal Francis Spellman, a reliable supporter of whatever war America was engaged in, had at times been under pressure to suppress the Catholic Worker, or at least to forbid use of the word "Catholic" in the title of its newspaper, but remarkably never did so. Perhaps he sensed that, in Dorothy Day, he had a saint in his diocese and that he had better not play the match-lighter's part in the trial of a modern-day Joan of Arc. Maybe he just sensed, puzzling though it must have been, that the church needed the Catholic Worker movement.

As the sixties began, Merton was not a controversial figure. His books were available in bookshops, libraries, drugstores, news-stands, train and bus terminals as well as churches, and each bore an *Imprimatur* (Latin for "let it be printed," a bishop's certification that the book was free of theological error). Many thousands owed their faith, and millions its deepening, to the stimulus of Merton's writings. His writings had been published in more languages than we had staff members and volunteers in our Catholic Worker house of hospitality. His books were read by the convinced and the unconvinced. His readers ranged from popes to prostitutes.

The letters from Merton that Dorothy shared with me were factors in the decision I made in April 1961 to take part, though not in uniform, in a protest of the CIA-sponsored Bay of Pigs invasion of Cuba. A week later, having found myself in very hot water with my commanding officer and the Naval Intelligence Service, I filed an application for early discharge from the Navy as a conscientious

Dorothy Day under arrest for civil
disobedience. (Photo: Robert Lax)

objector. The request was quickly granted. In late May, at Dorothy's
invitation, I became part of the Catholic Worker community in
New York.

If it is hard now to fully appreciate what Merton's letters meant to
their recipients, it may be harder still to understand the apocalyptic
worldview many people—Merton among them—had at the time.
No one following the headlines could reasonably expect to die of
old age. Many people today seem to have gotten used to living in
a world heavily stocked with nuclear weapons. The fact that none
have been used in warfare since the destruction of Hiroshima and
Nagasaki in August 1945 is seen as proof that deterrence works. In
the short measure of human life and memory, and in a time crowded

with other disasters, Hiroshima is a long way off. We have begun to count on generals and their subordinates restraining themselves from pressing the nuclear button. We imagine that, for the first time in human history, weapons are being produced and made ready for use—are in fact poised for use—yet will never be used. May it be so. Yet it didn't seem to Merton or those engaged with the Catholic Worker that human nature had changed since Hiroshima or that those who see reality in purely abstract ideological terms, a mentality not uncommon in political and military leadership, no matter what the nationality, could be counted on to leave nuclear weapons on the shelf if other methods failed to achieve the desired goal—or someone with a launch code gets a Doctor Strangelove itch to take "decisive action."

A small poster tacked to my apartment wall bore a four-word message: "Get ready to die." In 1961, when even monasteries were building fallout shelters, each time I heard New York's sirens being tested I expected to be shredded into radioactive particles. The sirens would begin their coordinated howling, the blasts punctuated by silences so severe the city suddenly seemed desert-like in stillness. Stunned, momentarily paralyzed by the significance of the noise, I would stop whatever I was doing in the Catholic Worker's third-floor office and wait at the front window, gathering a final view of our battered neighborhood with its few scarred trees struggling for light and air—even here, a kind of beauty. Shortly it would all be consumed by fire. There was no need to think about a hiding place. Even were there a massive barrier against the blast and radiation, the blast's firestorm would consume all the oxygen. Last moments are too important to be wasted. We were Christians who had done our best to take Jesus at his plain words in our awkward Catholic Worker way. We believed in the resurrection and hoped in God's mercy. Ours was a faith that seemed bizarre if not insane to many, but it gave these moments a certain tranquility, despite the sadness for this immense funeral we humans had so laboriously brought upon ourselves.

But each time the sirens ceased their doomsday howls. There was no sudden radiance brighter than a thousand suns. At such times I felt like an airline passenger setting shaking feet upon solid ground after a no-wheels landing in emergency foam spread out across the runway. Our lives had ended and been given back. We had in our hands another chance to free ourselves from a "security" founded upon the preparation of nuclear holocaust. Another chance for figs to grow from thistles.

Cover of *Liberation*

In July 1961 Dorothy received a letter from Merton that accompanied a poem about Auschwitz and the Holocaust—"Chant to Be Used in Procession around a Site with Furnaces." Merton had written it during the trial of Adolf Eichmann then going on in Jerusalem. In his letter Merton described the poem as a "gruesome" work. It was written in the staccato voice of Rudolf Höss, the commandant of Auschwitz, who catalogued the many efficiencies he had introduced to the concentration camp so that its assembly line might produce its quota of dead bodies:

> *How we made them sleep and purified them*
> *How we perfectly cleaned up the people and worked a big*
> *   heater . . .*
> *All the while I had obeyed perfectly.*

In its final razor-edged sentence, the mass-murderer's gaze turned from himself to the reader:

> *Don't think yourself better because you burn up friends and enemies*
> *with long-range missiles without ever seeing what you have done.*[4]

---

4. *Emblems of a Season of Fury* (ESF), 43-47.

It was thanks to the Auschwitz poem that my own correspondence with Merton had its genesis. Dorothy astonished me by handing me his letter and asking me to answer it. "Tell Father Louis [Merton's name as a monk] we will use the poem in the upcoming [August] issue—it will serve as our response to the Eichmann trial."

To my even greater amazement, Merton responded to my brief letter. The several paragraphs included news of how he had begun the day, August 9, anniversary of the nuclear destruction of Nagasaki:

This morning I said the Mass in Time of War. Might as well face it. [The text of the war-time mass] is a very good formulary. Nowhere in it are there promises of blessings upon the strong and the unscrupulous or the violent. Only suggestions that we shut up and be humble and stay put and trust in God and hope for a peace that we can use for the good of our souls. It is certainly not a very belligerent Mass, and it asks no one to be struck down. But it does say that we don't have to worry too much about the King of Babylon. Are we very sure he has his headquarters in Moscow only?[5]

Looking back, little in my experience of Dorothy Day impresses me so much as her willingness to open the door to a relationship between a young volunteer and so significant a friend. It may have been her way of encouraging my interest in a monastic vocation plus her awareness of my appreciation of Merton's books. Also she was increasingly involving me in the production of the paper.

In late September 1961 Dorothy received Merton's first-ever prose submission to *The Catholic Worker*, "The Root of War Is Fear." The phrase was familiar. One of the Merton books I had read while still in the Navy was *Seeds of Contemplation*, published in 1949, which included a chapter with the same title but in content quite different. Now twelve years later, the book had been expanded and substantially revised (an additional hundred pages were added) and rechristened *New Seeds of Contemplation*.[6]

---

5. HGL, 255.
6. *New Seeds of Contemplation* (NSC).

"The Root of War Is Fear," just four pages in the 1949 version, was now ten pages long. While retaining a fragment of the original material, the text was deeper and more developed. In it Merton stressed recognition of the human tendency to accuse the other rather than to accuse oneself, so that, failing to recognize our own co-responsibility for evils that lead toward war, we come to see war—even nuclear war—as necessary and justified. Merton wrote of the irony of the American government promoting "Pray for Peace" as a slogan (for years it was used for canceling postage stamps) while spending a "fabulous amount of money, planning, energy, anxiety and care" on the production of weapons of mass annihilation. "It does not even seem to enter our minds," Merton wrote, "that there might be some incongruity in praying to the God of peace, the God who told us to love one another as He had loved us, who warned us that they who took the sword would perish by it, and at the same time annihilate not thousands but millions of civilians and soldiers, women and children without discrimination." Only love, he wrote, "can exorcise the fear which is at the root of war."

Merton asked Dorothy if this might be something suitable for use in *The Catholic Worker*. Dorothy handed Merton's typescript to me, telling me to put in subheads and send it to the printer for typesetting. "Also write to Father Louis and tell him his article will be in the next issue."

In fact the text Merton sent Dorothy included several additional paragraphs especially written for the *Catholic Worker* version "to situate these thoughts in the present crisis." He wrote:

> *The present war crisis is something we have made entirely for and by ourselves. There is in reality not the slightest logical reason for war, and yet the whole world is plunging headlong into frightful destruction, and doing so with the purpose of avoiding war and preserving peace! This is true war-madness, an illness of the mind and spirit that is spreading with a furious and subtle contagion all over the world. Of all the countries that are sick, America is perhaps the most grievously afflicted. On all sides we have people building bomb shelters where, in case of nuclear war, they will simply bake slowly instead of burning*

quickly or being blown out of existence in a flash. And they are pre-pared to sit in these shelters with machine guns with which to prevent their neighbor from entering.[7]

As it happened, just as we were going to press with Merton's article, the *New York Times* gave front-page attention to an essay, "Ethics at the Shelter Doorway," that had been published in the Jesuit magazine *America*,[8] in which the theologian Father L. C. McHugh, S.J., justified just such a deadly response to improvident neighbors. McHugh argued: "If a man builds a shelter for his family, then it is the family that has the first right to use it. The right becomes empty if a misguided charity prompts a pitying house-holder to crowd his haven in the hour of peril, for this conduct makes sure that no one will survive." ("No doubt," Merton commented soon after, "the case could be made for St. Peter to kill St. Paul if there was only enough food for one of them to survive winter in a mountain cave.")

Merton's supplementary *Catholic Worker* text continued:

This in a nation that claims to be fighting for religious truth along with freedom and other values of the spirit. Truly we have entered the "post-Christian era" with a vengeance. Whether we are destroyed or whether we survive, the future is awful to contemplate.

Then came a challenge to become more than passive bystanders:

What is the place of the Christian in all this? Is he simply to fold his hands and resign himself for the worst, accepting it as the inescapable will of God and preparing himself to enter heaven with a sigh of relief?[9] *Should he open up the Apocalypse and run into the street to give everyone his idea of what is happening? Or, worse still, should he take a hard-headed and "practical" attitude about it and join in the madness of the war makers, calculating how, by a "first strike,"*

---

7. PFP, 11-13.

8. Issue dated September 30, 1961.

9. Merton's use of the masculine pronoun was standard for general second-person statements in that era, including by women writers, Dorothy Day among them.

Vol. XXVIII   No. 3   October, 1961   Subscriptions 25c Per Year   Price 1c

THE WORKER PRIESTS

By Anne Taillefer

"Man is a living paradox and the Incarnation—the Word made flesh—is the greatest paradox of all" (Henri de Lubac). Thus vocation, the call of the supernatural to the natural, the message of the Lord, when utterly pure and obediently heard is apt to surprise us shatteringly. Of all the strange vocations that of workerpriest may be among the most dispossessed.

The present Anglican bishop of Tanganyka, who was then Father Trevor Huddleston, one of the great fighters against apartheid in South Africa, once said: "the trial of the worker-priests is that of Joan of Arc". Strangely enough his words are echoed in a letter written by an eminent ecclesiastic, years ago, to Father Godin, one of the founders of the movement: "It is doubtful if the Catholic Church, the Catholic hierarchy, by itself would have the courage to operate this reform. God will have to help or to constrain it to do so."

In another letter the same ecclesiastic who may or may not have been Cardinal Suhard says: "The rechristianization of France and above all of its workers demands, to begin with, a radical reform of our society. The form of slavery called proletariat must first be abolished totally. . . . The

THE ROOT OF WAR

By Thomas Merton

The present war crisis is something we have made entirely for and by ourselves. There is in reality not the slightest logical reason for war, and yet the whole world is plunging headlong into frightful destruction, and doing so **with the purpose of avoiding war and preserving peace!** This is a true war-madness, an illness of the mind and the spirit that is spreading with a furious and subtle contagion all over the world. Of all the countries that are sick, America is perhaps the most grievously afflicted. On all sides we have people building bomb shelters where, in case of nuclear war, they will simply bake slowly instead of burning up quickly or being blown out of existence in a flash. And they are prepared to sit in these shelters with machine guns with which to prevent their neighbor from entering. This in a nation that claims to be fighting for religious truth along with freedom and other values of the spirit. Truly we have entered the "post-Christian era" with a vengeance. Whether we are destroyed or whether we survive, the future is awful to contemplate.

The Christian

What is the place of the Christian in all this? Is he simply to fold his hands and resign himself—

Cover of the October 1961 issue of *The Catholic Worker,* featuring "The Root of War."

the glorious Christian West can eliminate atheistic communism for all time and usher in the millennium? I am no prophet and seer but it seems to me that this last position may very well be the most diabolical of illusions, the great and not even subtle temptation of a Christianity that has grown rich and comfortable, and is satisfied with its riches.

Merton then addressed the question of making an appropriate response:

What are we to do? The duty of the Christian in this crisis is to strive with all his power and intelligence, with his faith, his hope in Christ, and love for God and man, to do the one task which God has imposed upon us in the world today. That task is to work for the total abolition of war. There can be no question that unless war is abolished the world will remain constantly in a state of madness and desperation in which, because of the immense destructive power of modern weapons, the danger of catastrophe will be imminent and probable at every moment everywhere. Unless we set ourselves immediately to this task, both as individuals and in our political and religious groups, we tend by our very passivity and fatalism to cooperate with the destructive forces that are leading inexorably to war. It is a problem of terrifying complexity and magnitude, for which the Church itself is not fully able to see clear and decisive solutions. Yet she must lead the way on the road to the nonviolent settlement of difficulties and toward the gradual abolition of war as the way of settling international or civil disputes. Christians must become active in every possible way, mobilizing all their resources for the fight against war. First of all there is much to be studied, much to be learned. Peace is to be preached, nonviolence is to be explained as a practical method, and not left to be mocked as an outlet for crackpots who want to make a show of themselves. Prayer and sacrifice must be used as the most effective spiritual weapons in the war against war, and like all weapons, they must be used with deliberate aim: not just with a vague aspiration for peace and security, but against violence and war. This implies that we are also willing to sacrifice and restrain our own instinct for violence and aggressiveness in our relations with other people. We may never succeed in this campaign, but whether we succeed or not, the duty is evident. It is the great Christian task of our time. Everything else is secondary, for the survival of the human race itself depends upon it. We must at least face this responsibility and do something about it. And the first job of all is to understand the psychological forces at work in ourselves and in society.

The expanded *Catholic Worker* version of this chapter, comments William Shannon in his anthology of Merton's social essays, *Passion for Peace*, "marked the initial and definitive entry of Thomas Merton into the struggle against war."[10] Notably, the additional text had not been vetted by Trappist censors.

We placed "The Root of War" essay on page 1 of the October issue alongside a line-drawing of Saint Francis of Assisi. The same day the issue was delivered from the printer, I sent out a press release that contrasted Merton's essay with Father McHugh's article in

---

10. PFP, 11.

America—probably the first Catholic Worker press release issued in many a year.

In a letter to me sent soon after receiving copies of the October issue, Merton said he had now read the McHugh article, which seemed to him scandalous:

> *Not that men renounce the right to defend themselves, but it is a question of emphasis and viewpoint. Are we going to ... fix our eyes on the lowest level of natural ethics, or are we going to be Christians and take the Gospel seriously.... Now is the chance for us to be Christians, and it may be the last chance. If we let this go, the world may be destroyed.... The big question is indeed to save the Christian faith, but if we strive to save it with bombs and nuclear submarines we are going to lose it. If we are going to save Christendom, there must be some Christendom to save, not just nominal Christianity.*

While not denying that violent methods of national defense may be necessary when nonviolent methods are impractical, Merton stressed the need to carefully explore the nonviolent alternative:

> *[We] have a serious obligation ... to investigate the meaning and feasibility of nonviolent defense not only on the individual but on the national level.... We have got to see things the way the Gospel sees them, the way the saints see them, the way the Church sees them, not just from the viewpoint of natural ethics....* [11]

Merton ended his letter with a request for another twenty copies of the October *Catholic Worker*.

Two days later Merton made a lengthy entry in his journal describing his sense of having crossed a border:

> *I am perhaps at a turning point in my spiritual life: perhaps slowly coming to a point of maturation and the resolution of doubts—and the forgetting of fears. Walking in to a known and definite battle. May God protect me in it. The Catholic Worker sent out a press release*

---

11. HGL, 256-57; letter dated October 21, 1961.

Dorothy Day with copies of the October 1961 issue of *The Catholic Worker*. (Marquette University Archives)

about my article, which may have many reactions—or may have none. At any rate it appears that I am one of the few Catholic priests in the country who has come out unequivocally for a completely intransigent fight for the abolition of war, for the use of nonviolent means to settle international conflicts. Hence by implication not only against the bomb, against nuclear testing, against Polaris [nuclear-armed] submarines but against all violence. This I will inevitably have to explain in due course. Nonviolent action, not mere passivity. How I am going to explain myself and defend a definite position in a timely manner when it takes at least two months to get even a short article through the censors of the Order is a question I cannot attempt to answer.

In a way I think the position of the Order is in fact unrealistic and absurd. That at a time like this no one in the Order should seem to be concerned with the realities of the world situation in a practical way—that monks in general, even those [Benedictines] who can speak out fully—are immersed in little scholarly questions about medieval writers and texts of minor importance even to scholars, and this is in the greatest moral crisis in the history of man: this seems to me incomprehensible. Especially when it is the definite policy of the Cistercian Order to impede and obstruct every expression of concern, every opinion, in published written form, that has reference to the crisis. This seems to me extremely grave. The futility of taking the issue up and solving it is evident; I talked to Fr. Clement, the [Abbot]

General's secretary about it, and it was like talking to a wall. Total incomprehension and lack of sympathy. The General himself is more understanding and Dom James[12] *too sees the point somewhat (they surprisingly released* Original Child Bomb *[Merton's poem about the atom bombs dropped on Hiroshima and Nagasaki] after the censors had definitively blocked it).*

And the Jesuit who condoned—even apparently encouraged—the business of sitting in your fallout shelter with a machine gun to keep others out! This is the best Catholic theology has had to offer in this country, so it appears.

At least I feel clean for having stated what is certainly the true Christian position. Not that self-defense is not legitimate, but there are wider perspectives than that and we have to see them. It is not possible to solve our problems on the basis of "every man for himself" and saving your own skin by killing the first person who threatens it. . . .

I am happy that I have turned a corner, perhaps the last corner in my life. The sense of abandon and home-going joy, love for the novices, whom I see as though dwelling in light and in God's blessing—as we go home together. And the thought is not negative or destructive—for it is a fulfillment, and whatever happens to the world, its infinitely varied dance of epiphanies continues: or is perhaps finally transfigured and perfected forever.[13]

In its November 25 issue, *America* published eleven pro and con letters responding to the McHugh article. The same month a follow-up essay by Merton, "The Shelter Ethic," was featured in *The Catholic Worker*. In it Merton argued that Christian responsibility involved more than building a shotgun-equipped fallout shelter:

It seems to me that at this time . . . instead of wasting our time in problematic ways of saving our own skin, we ought to be seeking with all our strength to act as better Christians, as men of peace, dedicated

---

12. Each abbey had its own abbot. The abbot general is the worldwide head of the Order.

13. TTW, 172-73; journal entry dated October 23, 1961.

Civil defense poster

wholeheartedly to the law of love which is the law of Christ.... We are in the midst of what is perhaps the most crucial moral and spiritual crisis the human race has ever faced during its history. We are all deeply involved in this crisis, and consequently the way each individual faces the crisis has a definite bearing on the survival of the whole race.... [W]hile each individual certainly retains the right to defend his life and protect his family, we run the risk of creating a very dangerous mentality and opening the way to moral chaos if we give the impression that from here on out it is just every man for himself, and the devil take the hindmost....

[L]et us get rid of this poisonous viewpoint that ... one is being noble and dutiful if one is ready to shoot his neighbor. There are higher ideals we can keep in mind. Let us not forget that the supreme example of nonviolent resistance to evil is the crucifixion of Our Lord Jesus Christ, in which the Incarnate Son of God destroyed sin by taking the sins of the world upon Himself and dying on the Cross, while forgiving the men who were putting Him to death. Far from being an act of mere helpless passivity, as Nietzsche and other moderns claim, this was a free and willing acceptation of suffering in the most positive and active manner. The activity in this case was hidden and spiritual. It was an exercise of the supremely dynamic spiritual force of divine love.

A Christian is committed to the belief that Love and Mercy are the most powerful forces on earth. Hence every Christian is bound by his baptismal vocation to seek, as far as he can, with God's grace, to make those forces effective in his life, to the point where they dominate all his actions. Naturally no one is bound to attain to the full perfection of charity. But a Christian who forgets that this is his goal, ceases by that fact to live and act as a genuine Christian. We must strive, then, to imitate Christ and His sacrifice, in so far as we are able. We must keep in mind His teaching that supreme love consists in laying down one's life for one's friends.

This means that a Christian will never simply allow himself to develop a state of mind in which, forgetting his Christian ideal, he thinks in purely selfish and pragmatic terms. Our rights certainly remain, but they do not entitle us to develop a hard-boiled, callous, selfish outlook, a "me first" attitude. This is that rugged individualism which is so unchristian and which modern movements in Catholic spirituality have so justly deplored.[14]

Civil defense poster

---

14. PFP, 21-26.

Meeting Merton

In December 1961 Merton invited me to come for a visit. In January, after getting the paper to press, I began to hitchhike to Kentucky with a poet friend and fellow Catholic Worker, Bob Kaye, bringing along a few loaves of still-warm bread from a Spring Street Italian bakery plus two small rucksacks of clothing. It was an exhausting three-day pilgrimage—long waits in remote places in inhospitable weather punctuated the last night with a few hours of uncomfortable sleep in the Indianapolis bus station. As we stood on the roadside with our numb thumbs in the air, armies of small plastic statues of Jesus of the Sacred Heart, his arms spread wide, blurred by us. The image of Christ's compassion and mercy attached to dashboards seemed to influence very few of the drivers. One of our hosts along the way was a drunk driver who, playing tag with death, miraculously brought us unharmed through a blizzard as Bob and I prayed our way to Gethsemani. Bob recalls me saying, "I would rather die in a warm car than freeze to death on the edge of the interstate."

When at last we arrived at the monastery and were shown to adjacent rooms in the guesthouse, Bob collapsed on his bed while I found my way through a connecting passageway to a balcony in the back of the monastery's barn-like church. Having survived the trip, a prayer of thanksgiving came easily, but it didn't last long. The church's silence was soon broken by distant laughter, a sound so intense and pervasive that I couldn't fail to be drawn to it. I wasn't in fact certain it was laughter, which seemed an improbable sound for a Trappist abbey. I quickly discovered the source was Bob's room. "Well, that's the difference between Bob and me," I thought. "I pray, and he gives way to laughter. God probably likes the laughter better." I pushed open the door, and indeed Bob was laughing, but the sound

Abbey of Gethsemane
(Courtesy Abbey of Gethsemane)

was mainly coming from a monk on the floor in his black and white robes, knees in the air, face bright red, hands clutching his belly. He was a shade more like Robin Hood's well-fed Friar Tuck than I imagined any fast-chastened Trappist could be—I had expected Merton to resemble the pencil-thin Ichabod Crane—but who else could this be than the author of so many books about such serious subjects, laughing himself half to death on the floor.

And laughing about what? While Bob must already have told a funny story or two from our thousand-mile journey, the most vivid answer came with my first gasp of air. The smell! Bob, after three days of rough travel without a change of socks, had taken off his shoes. The room was like the Fulton Fish Market in a heat wave. Had there ever been so rude a scent in this scrubbed monastery's history? It was, in a way, the Catholic Worker's social gospel incarnate—its unwashed vocation such as the church in all its cathedral glory had seldom seen since the first Franciscans seven centuries before. It made Merton roar with pleasure until the need to breathe took precedence and there could be a shaking of hands and a more traditional welcome.

He was still smiling as he left, telling us when we could get together later. As we parted I realized why his face, never seen before, as none of his books in those days carried the usual author photo, was nonetheless familiar: it was like Picasso's, as I had seen it in a book by David Duncan. Both faces were similarly unfettered in their expressiveness, eyes bright, quick and sure, suggesting mischief one moment and wisdom the next—unremarkable features on their own, but so remarkably animated in dialog.

I was impressed by his voice. Merton spoke plainly but with contagious feeling. Far from being pretentious or academic or piety personified, he reminded me of a cheerful truck driver—the kind of person who had sometimes given us rides on the way down.

Early in the visit I had my first glimpse of Merton's openness to non-Christians. It happened in the late afternoon on the first day I was there. There was a knock on the door of my room in the guesthouse. Merton was standing there, but in a rush as the bell was ringing for Vespers. He handed me a folder of papers that turned out to be a collection of Jewish Hasidic stories that a visiting rabbi, Zalman Schachter, had left with him a few days before. "Read this—these are great!" And off he hurried to Vespers without further explanation, leaving me with a collection of amazing tales of mystical Polish rabbis with souls on fire who had lived generations before the Holocaust.

I recall another meeting a day or two later when Merton was not in a rush. He was in good time for Vespers and already had on the white woolen choir robe the monks wore during winter months while in church. It was an impressive hooded garment, all the more

Thomas Merton
(Photo: John Howard Griffin)

striking at close range. I reached out to feel its thickness and density. In a flash Merton slid out of it and placed it over my head. I was unprepared for how heavy it was! Once again, Merton laughed. The robe met a practical need, he explained. It was hardly warmer in the church than it was outside. The chapel stove was lit only when a layer of ice had formed on the inside of the stained-glass windows. "If we wore only our black and white robes, on days like this we would freeze to death," Merton remarked.

The abbot, Dom James Fox, though a most hospitable man, was not initially quite so positive as Merton about a visitation of shaggy young Catholic Workers. In those days most American men had frequent haircuts, but haircuts seemed to Bob and me a massive waste of money. The morning of the second day Merton apologetically explained that our unshorn hair did not please Dom James. If we were to stay on at the abbey, we had to submit to haircuts. Merton hoped we wouldn't object. A little while later Bob and I took turns sitting in a barber chair in the basement room where the novices changed into their denim work clothes. While the novices stood in a circle laughing, our hair fell to the concrete floor. Going from one extreme to the other, I suddenly found myself as bald as a recruit on his first day at Boot Camp.

After the haircut, Merton took me to the abbot's office. On Dom James's desk was a copy of the latest *Catholic Worker* as well as several issues of the *Wall Street Journal*, not a combination one often encounters. He asked about Dorothy Day and community life at the Catholic Worker and what events had led me to the Catholic Church. I will never forget the solemn blessing Dom James gave me at the end of our conversation. "Would you like me to give you a blessing," he asked. Readily agreeing, I knelt on the floor near his desk while he gripped my skull while praying over me in Latin. He had a steel grip. I wouldn't be surprised if his fingerprints are still on my scalp. There was no doubt in my mind I had been seriously blessed. I have ever since had a warm spot in my heart for Dom James, a man who has occasionally been maligned by Merton biographers, assigned the role of Darth Vader to Merton's Luke Skywalker. It was obvious that, whatever tensions might have existed in his relationship with Merton, he had immense respect for him.

One monk who had much less sympathy for Merton was the abbey's other noted author, Father Raymond Flanagan, whose books were well known to Catholics at the time, though they never reached the wide audience Merton's books had. I came close to meeting Father Raymond one afternoon when Merton and I were walking down a basement corridor that linked the guesthouse kitchen to the basement of the main monastery building. There was a point in the corridor where it made a left turn. Standing there, next to a large garbage container, was an older monk who was not so much reading as glaring at the latest *Catholic Worker*, which he held open at arm's length as if the paper had an unpleasant smell. There was an article of Merton's in it, one of his essays about the urgency of taking steps to prevent nuclear war. Father Raymond looked up, saw us coming, balled the paper up in his fist, hurled it into the garbage container, and strode away without a word.

By this time I was getting used to Merton's laughter at unlikely times. He explained that Father Raymond had rarely had a high opinion of his writings and often reported Merton's faults at the community's chapter meetings at which infractions of the Benedictine Rule and Cistercian Usages were confessed or revealed. "When I first came here," Merton told me, "Father Raymond used to denounce me during the Chapter of Faults for being too hung up with contemplation and not concerned enough with the world. Now he denounces me for being too hung up with the world and not concerned enough with contemplation." (Apparently the tension between Merton and Father Raymond never abated. In March 1968, just eight months before his death, Merton recorded in his journal a furious verbal assault by Father Raymond, enraged with Merton's opposition to the war in Vietnam.[1])

At the time of the visit Merton was novice master, the person responsible for the education and spiritual formation of the novices. There were at least twenty of them at that time. Bob and I were invited to sit in with the novices in the classroom where Merton lectured and entered into discussion with the young monks. The topic at the time was contemplative theology. "I remember Merton's depth and his earthiness," Bob told me in a recent letter; "He was erudite, playful, elemental, matter of fact—a very, very practical man who, even if given to moments of poetry and lyrical beauty, spoke like a stevedore. Common sense: 'This is what these guys [this or that church father] say, this is the story, this is how we use it to sharpen our wits and soften our souls to the truth, this is how we stay sane. This is how you lay the brick.' He didn't use language carelessly or frivolously. There was no embroidery there."

At one class Merton wore a peace button that I had given him; he proceeded to explain the symbol—a circle bisected by a vertical line with two diagonal lines descending from the midpoint in opposing directions. It was a design that superimposed the semaphore signals for N and D—nuclear disarmament. "It's an elegant design," Merton pointed out to the novices, "with a simple message. Good for any monk to wear." The novices laughed and Merton with them.

The guest master, Father Francis, knew I was at the monastery at Merton's invitation and thought I might be able to answer a question that puzzled him and no doubt many of the monks: "How does Father Louis write all those books?" Of course I had no idea, even less than he did, but I got a glimpse of an answer before my stay was over. A friend who sometimes volunteered at the Catholic Worker, Allen Hoffman, had sent a letter to Merton in my care. Allen, though not Catholic, admired Merton's recent anti-war writings but hadn't a clue why he would "imprison" himself in a monastery which itself

---

1. *The Other Side of the Mountain* (OSM), 62; journal entry dated March 7, 1968.

Merton with the novices.
(Courtesy: Columbia University Butler Library)

was part of a church that was in such need of reform. He urged Merton to leave and do something "more relevant," such as join a Catholic Worker community and take part in campaigning for nuclear disarmament. What was most impressive to me about this particular letter was less its content or Merton's response but the experience of watching Merton write. He had a small office just outside the novitiate classroom. On his desk was a large grey Royal typewriter. He inserted a piece of monastery stationery and wrote a reply at what seemed to me the speed of light. I had never seen anyone write so quickly. You might sometimes see a skilled stenographer type at such speed when copying a text, but even in a city newsroom of that period one rarely saw anyone writing at a similar pace. The sheet of paper was in danger of bursting into flame.

I wish I had made a copy of his response. Allen died young, and the letter, if he kept it, was probably tossed out. I recall Merton readily admitted that there was much to reform both in monasteries and in the Catholic Church. He also said that monastic life was not a vocation to which God often called his children, yet he gave an explanation of why he thought the monastic life was nonetheless an authentic Christian vocation and how crucial it was for him to remain faithful to what God had called him to. It was a very solid, carefully reasoned letter filling one side of a sheet of paper and was written in just a few minutes.

I wasn't aware of it at the time, but for years Merton had been campaigning for greater solitude. In 1960, nearly a year before our visit, plans were made by Dom James for the construction of a compact cinder-block building. In theory this was to be a conference center where Merton could engage in dialog with small groups of visitors, but Merton called it his hermitage. It stood on the edge of the woods about a mile north of the monastery. Merton had lit the first fire in the fireplace on December 26, not many weeks before our arrival. There was a narrow bedroom behind the main room, its bed covered by a patchwork quilt. Merton occasionally had permission to stay overnight, but it would not be until the summer of 1965 that it became his full-time home. At that point he became the abbey's first Trappist hermit.

The hermitage already had a lived-in look when Bob and I saw it. It was winter so there was no sitting on the porch, but we stood there for a time gazing into the wet distance. Merton broke the silence to say, "God is raining." Once inside, Merton got a blaze going in the fireplace, the only source of heat. A supply of split logs was kept in a large basket on the left side of the hearth. A Japanese calendar hung on one wall with a Zen brush drawing for every month of the year, though the page being shown was long past. Also on the wall was a black-on-black painting by his friend from Columbia days, Ad Reinhardt. If looked at carefully, it revealed a cross. Three side-by-side windows provided a panoramic view of fields and distant hills. A long table behind the windows served as a desk. A bookcase stood next to it. On Merton's worktable was a handsome Swiss-made Hermes portable typewriter. A tall timber cross had been erected

Merton's hermitage. (Photo by Michael Plekhon)

on the lawn that had an iron-rimmed wagon wheel leaning against it. Off to one side of the hermitage was an outhouse that Merton shared with a black snake, a harmless but impressive creature. As yet, the hermitage had no kitchen or chapel and no running water or electricity—these were added several years later. There was a shallow closet in the bedroom. Merton opened the door to reveal on its inner side a certificate, at the top an oval portrait of the pope with a text below within many decorative swirls. The blessing was made out to "the hermit Thomas Merton" and was signed Paul VI.

In response to a question Bob had asked about the Mass while we sat talking in the hermitage, Merton spoke of the eucharistic liturgy being a kind of ritual dance at the crossroads, a place of encounter for every condition of people and every degree of faith, and also an intersection linking time and eternity.

Walking with him to the hermitage a day or two later, on this occasion just the two of us, I asked Merton to hear my confession, in the course of which I talked with him about a question that had been haunting me for many months: should I "try my vocation" (that was the phrase used in those days) as a monk—and, if so, did he think I should do it at the Abbey of Gethsemani? I told him of the negative advice I had been given at another Trappist monastery, Saint Joseph's in Massachusetts, and a similar response I had gotten by letter from a Benedictine monk at Saint John's Abbey in Minnesota. In both cases the fact of my having left the military as a conscientious objector was seen as an indication that I was not a good fit. The monk at Saint Joseph's had remarked, "We find that those who don't do well in the military tend not to do well in monastic life." Merton smiled. "In some monasteries they might elect you abbot for the same reason, but not in America. You would think it would be a good sign if an applicant was opposed to war! There was a time when you couldn't get baptized unless you promised not to kill people. Well, you are certainly welcome to come here and enter the novitiate and see if you are cut out for Trappist life, but somehow I think the path you are already on may be where God intends you to be. Right now the church needs people working for peace in a way that's impossible here—the kind of things you're doing at the Catholic Worker. If you want to try the life, it's possible and I would be glad to have you, but wait a while. I think the Holy Spirit has other things in mind."

During our visit the latest copy of *Jubilee* arrived. *Jubilee* was a monthly journal edited by Ed Rice, Merton's friend from their days at Columbia and also his godfather. Rice had the collaboration of a small, committed staff of talented, underpaid colleagues, one of whom was Bob Lax. Merton was among the magazine's advisors, cheerlead-

Interior of the hermitage.
(Photo by Jim Forest)

ers, and notable writers. In the years it existed, 1953 to 1967, *Jubilee* was unique among Catholic magazines. There wasn't a single issue that failed to be arresting—impressive photo features plus some of the most striking layouts and typography of the time. The content was wide ranging, with profiles and interviews with remarkable people, vivid features on church life, portraits of houses of hospitality, well-illustrated articles on liturgy, art, and architecture, and occasional glimpses of the Orthodox Christian world. In that particular issue was a set of photos showing life in an Orthodox monastery on Mount Athos in Greece. One of the photos was of a heavily-bearded monk who looked old enough to have known Abraham. He was standing behind a long battered table in the refectory, while behind him was a fresco of the Last Judgment. The monk's head was bowed slightly. His eyes seemed to contain the cosmos. There was a remarkable stillness and vulnerability in his face. "Look at him," Merton said. "This guy has been kissed by God."[2]

Our stay ended abruptly. A telegram came from New York with the news that President Kennedy had announced the resumption of open-air testing of nuclear weapons in response to a similar decision made by Soviet leader Nikita Khrushchev, thus another escalation of the Cold War and yet another indication that nuclear war might well occur in the coming years. Anticipating Kennedy's decision, Bob and I had been part of a group of New Yorkers who had prepared an act of civil disobedience, a sit-in at the entrance to the Manhattan office of the Atomic Energy Commission, the federal agency then responsible for making and testing nuclear weapons.

Dom James provided money for our return to New York by bus rather than thumb. A few days later I was in a Manhattan jail known to New Yorkers as The Tombs. Singling me out as a "ringleader," an irritated judge sent me to Hart Island Prison for fifteen days. (With

---

2. For a detailed portrait of the Merton–Rice–Lax friendship as well as a history of *Jubilee* magazine, see James Harford, *Merton and Friends* (New York: Continuum, 2006).

my almost-bald Gethsemani haircut plus smiling face, a photo of me being carried to a police van was striking enough to be placed on the front page of one of New York's tabloid newspapers the day after the action.)

Merton had a part even in that event at the Atomic Energy Commission. A letter from him, sent care of the Catholic Worker, was hand-delivered to me during the hour or two that we sat on the icy pavement awaiting arrest.

The letter began, "If you are not in jail," then proposed publication in *The Catholic Worker* of a new essay that he enclosed with the letter.

"Christian Ethics and Nuclear War"[3] appeared in the March 1962 issue. In it Merton observed that many American Catholics were confusing the interests of the West and NATO with the interests of the church, assuming that U.S.-led Western society equals Christendom while Soviet Communism equals the Antichrist. Thus "we are ready to declare without hesitation that 'no price is too high' to pay for our religious liberty" without grasping that in fact that no one, least of all Christians, "has the right to take measures that may destroy millions of innocent noncombatants." Yet one readily found Christians who regarded initiating nuclear war against Soviet Russia as a holy crusade, an act they dared to imagine would be blessed by God. In fact, Merton wrote:

> *It is absurd and immoral to pretend that Christendom can be defended by the H[ydrogen]-bomb. As Saint Augustine would say, the weapon with which we would attempt to destroy the enemy would pass through our own hearts to reach him. We would be annihilated morally. . . .* [4]

---

3. PFP, 56-64.

4. The text is also included in *Peace in the Post-Christian Era* (PPCE), in the chapter "Theologians and Defense."

Merton's Collision with Censors

SINCE THE REFORMATION, censorship had been deeply embedded in Catholic life. A Catholic writing on theological topics was required to submit his or her books for scrutiny to an official censor who might in time grant a declaration of *nihil obstat* (Latin for "without error"), which would clear the way for the local bishop to give the book his *imprimatur* ("let it be printed"). For a Trappist author, the process was still more complex, involving prior approbation by censors within the order before the monk's abbot gave permission for the book to be forwarded to the bishop for final approval. For the Trappists, it was not enough that a book or article be free of theological error; the topic also had to be deemed suitable for a Trappist to address. The Trappist upper echelon was dominated by Gaullists who favored France's entry into the "nuclear club." "The abbots general in the fifties and sixties kept an eagle eye on Merton's writings," one older Trappist told me. "Their view was that prayer and weeping, not social commentary, were the province of monks."

Following publication of "The Root of War Is Fear" in the October 1961 *Catholic Worker*, the first three paragraphs of which had not been submitted to Trappist censors, censorship became a frequent topic in Merton's letters. It became increasingly difficult for him to get his war-and-peace-related articles into print, as some of the monks appointed as censors considered Merton's views on war inappropriate if not outrageous.

There is a document in the archive of the Thomas Merton Center in Louisville that gives a sense of the opposition Merton was facing within the Trappist order after October 1961. Here we have an unnamed abbot of another American Trappist community writing to the abbot general in Rome, Dom Gabriel Sortais, warning him of the scandal being caused by Merton's anti-war writings:

> *There is one further matter, Reverend Father, which I hesitate to speak of but which I feel I should. We have, in the United States, a weekly paper [in fact monthly] called "The Catholic Worker." This is a very radical paper, which some Americans believe is a tool of the Communists. Fr. Louis (under the name Thomas Merton) has been writing for it frequently. . . . The name "Thomas Merton" is almost synonymous in America with "Trappist." Thus quite a number of people believe that he is expressing the Trappist outlook. . . .*

The writer goes on to report that a military intelligence officer had visited his monastery and had spoken with him "concerning Father Louis." He concludes his letter by acknowledging that many have benefitted from Merton's "spiritual works," but:

> *[I]t is difficult to understand how [Father Louis] can express himself so strongly on questions as to whether the United States should test nuclear weapons and also the wisdom of building fallout shelters. It is hard to see how—as an enclosed religious—he has access to enough facts to pass a prudent judgment on such matters.*

It is unlikely that this was the only such letter sent to the abbot general. Similar criticism was made in an editorial published in an archdiocesan newspaper, *The Washington Catholic Standard*. Here Merton was described "as an absolute pacifist" whose recent writings ignored "authoritative Catholic utterances" and made "unwarranted charges about the intention of our government towards disarmament." (Presumably the editorial was written by the editor, Auxiliary Bishop Philip Hannan, a former military chaplain who later became archbishop of New Orleans. At the Second Vatican Council, Hannan would oppose the condemnation of nuclear weapons.)

Even prior to my first visit, Merton had written to me of the need "to work out something sensible on this absurd censorship deal." He discussed the subject with jarring candor:

> *The censorship is completely and deliberately obstructive, not aimed at combing out errors at all, but purely and simply preventing the publi-*

cation of material that "doesn't look good." And this means anything that ruffles in any way the censors' tastes or susceptibilities. . . .

That is the kind of thing one has to be patient with. It is wearying, of course. However, it is all I can offer to compare with what you people [at the Catholic Worker] are doing to share the lot of the poor. A poor man is one who has to sit and wait and wait and wait, in clinics, in offices, in places where you sign papers, in police stations, etc. And he has nothing to say about it. At least there is an element of poverty for me too. The rest of what we have here isn't that hard or that poor.[1]

Perhaps because it was poetry, *Original Child Bomb*[2] managed to squeeze past the censors. The title was a translation of the name that the Japanese gave to the new sort of weapon that had destroyed Hiroshima and Nagasaki. In forty-one stark sections, Merton narrated the story of how the "original child" had come into being and then been put to use. The text read like a scrapbook of newspaper clippings whose desert-dry voice suggested the death of conscience. The book's grim subtitle: "points for meditation to be scratched on the wall of a cave." Section 32 reads:

> *The bomb exploded within 100 feet of the aiming point. The fireball was 18,000 feet across. The temperature at the center of the fireball was 100,000,000 degrees. The people who were near the center became nothing. The whole city was blown to bits and the ruins all caught fire instantly everywhere. Burning briskly. 70,000 people were killed right away or died within a few hours. Those who did not die at once suffered great pain. Few of them were soldiers.*[3]

---

1. TM to JF, January 5, 1962; HGL, 260-61.
2. *Original Child Bomb* (OCB).
3. In May 1964 several *Hibakusha* (survivors of the bombing of Hiroshima and Nagasaki) visited Merton. In a journal entry, he describes them as "people signed

ORIGINAL CHILD BOMB

Cover of *Original Child Bomb*

Censorship problems forced Merton to remove his name as editor of another book, *Breakthrough to Peace*,[4] a collection of twelve essays on the threat of nuclear war. The illustrations included a map of New York City and the surrounding region showing rings of destruction in the event a fifty-megaton nuclear weapon were to explode over Wall Street. The zone of total destruction, the innermost circle, included all of Manhattan, Brooklyn, Queens, Bronx, and Newark.

"Target Equals City," an essay written in February 1962 and slated for publication in *The Catholic Worker,* was refused approval by his order's censors, the first of Merton's war-related writings to suffer that fate. In it he argued that a major ethical border had been crossed during the Second World War. On the Allies' side, it was a war that had begun with "a just cause if ever there was one." There was no doubt that Hitler was the aggressor in Europe and that Japan was in Asia. But by the war's end in 1945, not only Germany but the Allies had moved from bombing military targets to targeting whole cities. Those theologians who took church teaching on war seriously were forced to consider the question "whether the old [just war] doctrine [still] had any meaning."

---

and marked by the cruelty of this age, signs on their flesh because of the *thoughts of other men*" (*Dancing on the Waters of Life* [DWL], 104-5). For a more thorough treatment of the place Hiroshima had in Merton's life, see Patrick O'Connell's Hiroshima entry in *The Thomas Merton Encyclopedia,* ed. William Shannon, Christine Bochen, and Patrick O'Connell (Maryknoll, NY: Orbis Books, 2002).

4. *Breakthrough to Peace* (BTP). See Michael Mott, *The Seven Mountains of Thomas Merton* (Boston: Houghton Mifflin, 1984), 373-74, for details about getting *Breakthrough to Peace* into print. Though not identified as editor, Merton wrote the book's introduction.

The obliteration bombing of cities on both sides, culminating in the total destruction of Hiroshima and Nagasaki by one plane with one bomb for each, had completely changed the nature of war. Traditional standards no longer applied because . . . there was no longer any distinction made between civilian and combatant. . . . [In fact] the slaughter of civilians was explicitly intended as a means of "breaking enemy morale" and thus breaking the "will to resist." This was pure terrorism, and the traditional doctrine of war excluded such immoral methods. . . . These methods were practiced by the enemy [at the war's start, but by the time] the war ended they were bequeathed to the western nations.[5]

Merton recalled how, early in the war, Britain had declared that it would not imitate Germany's savage blitz-bombing tactics but instead would limit its bombing raids to military objectives. But in 1942 Britain abandoned its early restraint and began to target whole cities. "There are no lengths in violence to which we will not go," Churchill declared. To quiet troubled consciences, the argument was put forward that city destruction, in the long run, "will save lives and end the war sooner." In one notorious case, a thousand British and U.S. bombers dropped so many bombs on the German city of Dresden that a firestorm was created that gutted the heart of the city. An estimated 25,000 people were killed, including many refugees and Allied prisoners of war.[6] Far more died or were injured in the saturation bombing of Tokyo—the Tokyo Fire Department estimated 97,000 killed and 125,000 wounded.

Merton noted that while one can understand how those who suffered the Blitz would accept similar combat strategies against their enemy, no one could any longer claim that the standards of the just war doctrine, requiring not only a just cause but just methods that shelter noncombatant lives, were being respected.

The development of nuclear weapons and rockets for their deliv-

---

5. The essay was published only after Merton's death (PFP, 27-36).

6. One of the survivors was an American captive, Kurt Vonnegut. He later wrote of his near-death experience in Dresden in his sardonic novel *Slaughterhouse Five.*

ery to distant targets, many of which were cities, meant that city destruction had become an integral element of future war planning. While the policy is called deterrence, the effectiveness of deterrence depends on the demonstrated readiness to commit the gravest war crime ever contemplated.

Survivors of the blast at Nagasaki

Meanwhile the vast majority of Christians were offering no resistance. "The Christian moral sense is being repeatedly eroded," Merton wrote. When occasional protests occur or questions arise, "soothing answers are provided by policy makers and religious spokesmen are ready to support them with new [moral] adjustments. A new cycle is prepared. Once again there is a 'just cause.' Few stop to think that what is regarded complacently as 'justice' was clearly a crime twenty years ago. How long can Christian morality go on taking this kind of beating?"

Merton finished the essay with three sentences similar to those with which it had begun:

> There is only one winner in war. The winner is not justice, not liberty, not Christian truth. The winner is war itself.

A few months later Merton faced a much harder test. It was no longer a matter of enduring the delays and irritations of censorship, or the watering down or qualifying of his writing that this might involve, or the blocking of a particular essay. Now it was a matter of being forbidden to publish any war-related writings because, said Dom Gabriel, writing about war and peace "*fausserait le message de la vie contemplative*"—falsifies the message of the contemplative life.[7]

---

7. Merton quoted the original French phrase in a letter to Jacques Maritain dated February 12, 1963; Thomas Merton, *The Courage for Truth: Letters to Writers* (CFT), 36.

In a letter dated April 29, 1962,[8] two days after receiving the order, Merton wrote at length to me about this:

> *I have been trying to finish my book on peace* [Peace in the Post-Christian Era], *and have succeeded in time for the axe to fall.*[9] *...* *Now here is the axe. For a long time I have been anticipating trouble with the higher superiors and now I have it. The orders are, no more writing about peace. This is transparently arbitrary and uncomprehending, but doubtless I have to make the best of it. ... In substance I am being silenced on the subject of war and peace. This I know is not a very encouraging thing. It implies all sorts of very disheartening consequences as regards the whole cause of peace. It reflects an astounding incomprehension of the seriousness of the present crisis in its religious aspect. It reflects insensitivity to Christian and Ecclesiastic values, and to the real sense of the monastic vocation. The reason given is that this is not the right kind of work for a monk, and that it "falsifies the monastic message." Imagine that: the thought that a monk might be deeply enough concerned with the issue of nuclear war to voice a protest against the arms race, [this] is supposed to bring the monastic life into disrepute. Man, I would think that it might just possibly salvage a last shred of repute for an institution that many consider to be dead on its feet. That is really the most absurd aspect of the whole situation, that these people insist on digging their own grave and erecting over it the most monumental kind of tombstone.*

Beneath the surface of the disagreement between Merton and his abbot general was a different conception of the identity and mission of the church and of the monastics within it. For Merton the monk was obliged to be among those most attentive to what was going on in the world at large and raise a prophetic voice in times of crisis:

---

8. Dom James Fox had received the order in January but for unexplained reasons held off for three months before giving it to Merton. It may be that in this period Dom James was attempting to change the abbot general's mind.

9. The book was finally published by Orbis Books in 2004, forty-two years after it was written.

Ruins of Dresden

The problem, from the point of view of the Church and its mission, is of course this. The validity of the Church depends precisely on spiritual renewal, uninterrupted, continuous, and deep. Obviously this renewal is to be expressed in the historical context, and will call for a real spiritual understanding of historical crises, an evaluation of them in terms of their inner significance and in terms of man's growth and the advancement of truth in man's world: in other words, the establishment of the "kingdom of God." The monk is the one supposedly attuned to the inner spiritual dimension of things. If he hears nothing, and says nothing, then the renewal as a whole will be in danger and may be completely sterilized. But these authoritarian minds believe that the function of the monk is not to see or hear any new dimension, simply to support the already existing viewpoints precisely insofar as and because they are defined for him by somebody else. Instead of being in the advance guard, he is in the rear with the baggage, confirming all that has been done by the officials. The function of the monk, as far as renewal in the historical context goes, then becomes simply to affirm his total support of officialdom. He has no other function, then, except perhaps to pray for what he is told to pray for: namely the purposes and the objectives of an ecclesiastical bureaucracy. The monastery as dynamo concept goes back to this. The monk is there to generate spiritual power that will justify over and over again the already pre-decided rightness of the officials above him. He must under no event and under no circumstances assume a role that implies any form of spontaneity and originality. He must be an eye that sees nothing except what is carefully selected for him to see. An ear that hears nothing except what it is advantageous for the managers for him to hear. We know what Christ said about such ears and eyes.

Finally he addressed the issue of whether or not to obey:

Now you will ask me: how do I reconcile obedience, true obedience (which is synonymous with love) with a situation like this? Shouldn't I just blast the whole thing wide open, or walk out, or tell them to jump in the lake?

Let us suppose for the sake of argument that this was not completely excluded. Why would I do this? For the sake of the witness for peace? For the sake of witnessing to the truth of the Church, in its reality, as against this figment of the imagination? Simply for the sake of blasting off and getting rid of the tensions and frustrations in my own spirit, and feeling honest about it?

In my own particular case, every one of these would backfire and be fruitless. It would be taken as a witness against the peace movement and would confirm these people in all the depth of their prejudices and their self-complacency. It would reassure them in every possible way that they are incontrovertibly right and make it even more impossible for them ever to see any kind of new light on the subject. And in any case I am not merely looking for opportunities to blast off. I can get along without it.

I am where I am. I have freely chosen this state, and have freely chosen to stay in it when the question of a possible change arose. If I am a disturbing element, that is all right. I am not making a point of being that, but simply of saying what my conscience dictates and doing so without seeking my own interest. This means accepting such

*limitations as may be placed on me by authority, and not because
I may or may not agree with the ostensible reasons why the limitations are imposed, but out of love for God who is using these things to
attain ends which I myself cannot at the moment see or comprehend.
I know He can and will in His own time take good care of the ones
who impose limitations unjustly or unwisely. That is His affair and
not mine. In this dimension I find no contradiction between love and
obedience, and as a matter of fact it is the only sure way of transcend-
ing the limits and arbitrariness of ill-advised commands.*[10]

Very strong stuff—one could fry a breakfast of bacon and eggs
on that letter. Given the ferocity of Merton's critique, the last seg-
ment came as a surprise. Obey an
unjust order? Is there not a place for
disobedience even in monastic life?
Few people in the peace movement
then or now could understand or
appreciate obedience in such circumstances, yet it was the kind of
decision that would be respected
and valued by Francis of Assisi or
Dorothy Day. It was in this area
that Merton's own nonviolence was
put to its hardest personal test. His
nonviolence implied "enduring all
things" that a transformation might
occur in which his adversaries were

(Courtesy Columbia University
Butler Library)

won over rather than made into objects of scandal or ridicule. Perhaps he recognized in the fears of his superiors the same fears that
existed elsewhere in the world, the fears that eventually give rise to
war. What would be the sense of calling others to patience in the
labors of safeguarding life when he couldn't be patient with opponents, his brothers, within his own community? The big question

10. TM to JF, April 29, 1962; HGL, 266-68.

for Merton was "whose minds would be changed" by his disobedience? In the wider public, those who agreed with Merton's out-of-step views on war would be confirmed in their view that the Catholic Church was an enemy of conscience, while many of those who disagreed would conclude that Merton, a disobedient monk, was being "used by the Communists."

Nonetheless Merton didn't respond passively. He quickly appealed to the abbot general, but the order was affirmed. He wrote to me in June:

> *I was denounced to him by an American abbot who was told by a friend in the intelligence service that I was writing for a "communist controlled publication"* [The Catholic Worker]. *You didn't know you were Communist controlled, did you? Maybe George* [a Catholic Worker volunteer who had recently visited Gethsemani] *is really Khrushchev's nephew. Meanwhile, though I look through all my pockets, I cannot find that old* [Communist Party] *card. Must have dropped out when I was mopping my brow in the confessional.*[11]

It was Abbot Dom James who saw a loophole in the silencing order. If Merton was prohibited from writing about war for book publishers, limited publication on a small scale was another matter. With Dom James's permission, a mimeographed edition of *Peace in the Post-Christian Era,* for controlled distribution to friends, was run off, the first printing followed not long afterward by a second.

By the end of 1962 there were five or six hundred copies of the book in circulation. Hot item that it was, few of them stayed long at any one address. Within a few months Merton's banned book must have reached thousands of attentive readers, many of them people of influence.

---

11. TM to JF, June 14, 1962; HGL, 268-69.

Peace in the Post-Christian Era

IN THE COURSE OF THE SUMMER of 1962, by which time I was on the New York staff of Catholic Relief Services, Merton sent me at least twenty copies of *Peace in the Post-Christian Era* to distribute. I still have one of them. I can see from marginal notes in it that I shared it with at least one other reader.

I was startled by the book's title. Were we really living in a *post-Christian* world? Most Americans professed belief in God, a great many identified themselves as Christian, and one didn't have to travel far to find well-attended churches. On reflection, however, I realized it wasn't easy to find Christians whose lives in some way were shaped by such basic teachings of Jesus as love of enemies or even a readiness to forgive.

In the text of his banned book Merton explained his use of the term:

> *Whether we like it or not, we have to admit we are already living in a post-Christian world, that is to say a world in which Christian ideals and attitudes are relegated more and more to the minority.... It is frightening to realize that the façade of Christianity which still generally survives has perhaps little or nothing behind it, and that what was once called "Christian society" is more purely and simply a materialistic neo-paganism with a Christian veneer.*[1] ...
>
> *Not only non-Christians but even Christians themselves tend to dismiss the Gospel ethic on nonviolence and love as "sentimental."*[2]

I no longer have a copy of my letter to Merton responding to my first reading of the book, nor has it survived in the Merton archives

---

1. In the chapter "Religious Problems of the Cold War" (PPCE, 72).
2. In the chapter "Beyond East and West" (PPCE, 92).

in Louisville, but I see from a reply Merton sent me on July 7 that I put forward a number of suggestions for revision in the event the ban was lifted and he was able to do more work on *Peace in the Post-Christian Era*. I recall expressing disappointment that Merton's personal convictions about war, so vividly described in *The Seven Storey Mountain*, were not expressed more explicitly in *Peace in the Post-Christian Era*. I proposed that he add a section about Francis of Assisi, a saint particularly important to Merton.

Merton wrote in reply:

> *Thanks for your remarks on the book. That just goes to show what a mess one gets into trying to write a book that will get through the censors, and at the same time say something. I was bending in all directions to qualify every statement and balance everything off, so I stayed right in the middle and perfectly objective . . . [at the same time trying] to speak the truth as my conscience wanted it to be said. In the long run the result is about zero. . . .*
>
> *Certainly if I ever get to work over the book again, I will bear in mind your requests. At the moment the best I can do is . . . run off some more copies of what there is already. I have about a dozen copies left . . . and was more or less holding on to them in case special requests came in from people who had chance of borrowing a copy.*[3]

Reading this letter again after all these years, I am struck by how the white-hot anger regarding his silencing that Merton had vented in his April letter had either cooled or been put under wraps. I'm also impressed by his stunning modesty in his reply to a reader not half his age. Yet in that period one sees in Merton's journal entries and letters to other friends how hard the struggle was to come to terms with being gagged on what he remained convinced was a life-and-death issue toward which Christians could not turn a blind eye. Certainly he did not believe that he had been wasting his time in writing the book, nor could he agree that it was just as well that it went unpublished.

---

3. HGL, 263; letter dated July 7, 1962.

Atomic explosion over Nagasaki

What was the banned book all about? At its core was the urgency of outlawing total war—wars of city destruction—and banning nuclear and other weapons (biological and chemical) being made ready for use in such a war:

> *I wish to insist above all on one fundamental truth: that all nuclear war, and indeed massive destruction of cities, populations, nations and cultures by any means whatever, is a most serious crime which is forbidden to us not only by Christian ethics but by every sane and serious moral code.*[4]

---

4. In the chapter "Can We Choose Peace?" (PPCE, 19).

Even the use of less powerful "tactical" nuclear weapons, Merton argued, opens the way to total war "when we remember that the twenty kiloton A-bomb that was dropped on Hiroshima is now regarded . . . as a 'tactical device' and when we keep in mind that there is every probability that a force that is being beaten with small nuclear weapons will resort to big ones."

Merton reminded his readers that at the core of Christianity is respect for the life of the other, whether friend or enemy:

> *The doctrine of the Incarnation makes the Christian obligated at once to God and to man. If God has become man, then no Christian is ever allowed to be indifferent to man's fate. Whoever believes that Christ is the Word made flesh believes that every man must in some sense be regarded as Christ. For all are at least potentially members of the Mystical Christ. . . .*
>
> *The Christian responsibility is not to one side or the other in the power struggle: it is to God and truth, and to the whole of mankind. . . .*
>
> *Even if the other shows himself to be unjust, wicked and odious to us, we cannot take upon ourselves a final and definitive judgment in his case. We still have an obligation to be patient, and to seek his highest spiritual interests. . . . The love of enemies . . . [is] an expression of eschatological faith in the realization of the messianic promises and hence a witness to an entirely new dimension in man's life. . . . The Christian is and must be by his very adoption as a son of God, in Christ, a peacemaker (Matt 5:9). He is bound to imitate the Savior who, instead of defending Himself with twelve legions of angels (Matt 26:55), allowed Himself to be nailed to the Cross and died praying for his executioners. . . .*
>
> *The Christian does not need to fight and indeed it is better that he should not fight, for insofar as he imitates his Lord and Master, he proclaims that the Messianic kingdom has come and bears witness to the presence of the* Kyrios Pantocrator *[Lord of Creation] in mystery even in the midst of the conflicts and turmoil of the world.*[5]

---

5. In the chapter "The Christian as Peacemaker" (PPCE, 27-33).

Merton was appalled by the passivity with which American Christians, Catholics not least among them, viewed nuclear war with fatalism and in many cases even advocated it:

> *There is still all too general an apathy and passivity among the clergy and the faithful. Perhaps it is exact to say that they are afflicted with a kind of moral paralysis. Hypnotized by the mass media, which tend to be aggressive and bellicose, baffled and intimidated by the general atmosphere of [Cold War] suspicion, [and] bewildered by the silence or the ambiguity of their pastors and religious leaders . . . people tend to withdraw into a state of passive and fatalistic desperation. There they have been literally run to earth by the shelter salesmen, and have set themselves despondently to digging holes in their back yards against the day when the missiles begin to fly.[6]*

Merton explored the history of the Christian response to war in the first several centuries, when refusal to take part in war was as normal as the refusal to regard the emperor as a god, and the gradual development of a "just war" theology, a doctrine initially sketched out by Saint Augustine in the fifth century of the Christian era.

> *[Theologians of the early Church such as Origen] took for granted that the Christian is a pacifist. Augustine, on the contrary, pleads with the soldier Boniface not to retire to the monastery but to remain in the army and do his duty, defending the North African cities menaced by barbarian hordes.*
>
> *In these two hundred years, there have been two events of outstanding importance: the Battle of the Milvian bridge in 312, leading to the conversion of Constantine and his official recognition of Christianity, and then, in 410, the fall of Rome before the onslaught of Alaric the Goth. When Augustine developed his theories of the "just war," the barbarians were at the gates of the city of Hippo, where he was bishop. . . . Augustine saw the shattered and collapsing Empire attacked on all sides by barbarian armies. War could not be avoided.*

---

6. In the chapter "Theologians and Defense" (PPCE, 88).

*The question was, then, to find out some way to fight that did not vio-
late the Law of Love.*

Augustine solved the problem by distinguishing intention from
action:

> *How does Augustine justify the use of force...? The external act
> may be one of violence. War is regrettable indeed. But if one's inte-
> rior motive is purely directed to a just cause and to love of the enemy,
> then the use of force is not unjust. This distinction between the external
> act and the interior intention is entirely characteristic of Augustine.
> "Love" he says, "does not exclude wars of mercy waged by the good"
> (Letter 138).*
>
> *"Love does not exclude wars of mercy waged by the good!" The
> history of the Middle Ages, of the Crusades, of the religious wars has
> taught us what evil could have been expected from this noble principle.
> Augustine, for all his pessimism about human nature, did not foresee
> the logical results of his thought....*
>
> *And so ... for centuries we have heard kings, princes, bishops,
> priests, ministers, and the Lord alone knows what variety of unctu-
> ous beadles and sacrists, earnestly urging all men to take up arms out
> of love and mercifully slay their enemies (including other Christians)
> without omitting to purify their interior intention. This, in fact, has
> been carried to such incredible extremes as to constitute one of the
> more enormous scandals in the story of Christendom. The fact that it
> still goes on, without respite, without compunction, without the bless-
> ing of even the slightest awareness of implicit ironies, is one of the most
> depressing features of Christian justifications of nuclear war.*[7]

Over the centuries, Merton continued, an elaborate doctrine
developed that spelled out the conditions that were required for a
war to be regarded as just and Christians permitted, if not required,
to fight in it: it must be a defensive war declared by legitimate
authority in which force is strictly limited and the greatest care is

---

7. In the chapter "War in Origen and Augustine" (PPCE, 39, 42-43).

taken to protect the rights and the lives of noncombatants and even of combatants.

Unfortunately, Merton noted, "history teaches us that these requirements were seldom met with in practice." One searches in vain to find the hierarchy of any nation at war—for example, the German Catholic hierarchy during the Hitler period—declaring as unjust the wars its members were fighting in.

Catholic moralists in the past, Merton pointed out, often stressed what was called "double effect" to justify the killing of noncombatants, so long as their deaths were unintended (in current military terminology "collateral damage"):

> *The principle of "double effect" was developed and used in some measure to help keep the power politics of . . . princes in concord with at least a bare minimum of Christian morality. According to this principle, an end which is in itself not evil, and which is directed by means that are not evil, may be pursued even if evil side-effects accidentally occur, provided they are not directly willed.*
>
> *The classic example of double effect given in the moral theologies of the seventeenth and eighteenth centuries is this: You are fleeing for your life on horseback. To save yourself you must ride through a narrow place and there is a child lying in the path. Saving your life is a good end; there is nothing evil about riding a horse. There is no other avenue of escape. It is unfortunate that you have to ride over the child. This may mean injuring him or even killing him. You do not directly will his death but the fact that the child is there does not place you under any moral obligation to renounce your own safety. Hence you can go on, and even if the child is killed you are not held morally responsible.*
>
> *This is of course an example of casuistry, and it obviously shows why casuistry has a bad name. We might ask if that bad name is not in some respects perfectly justified. The moral casus conscientiae [case of conscience] was originally devised, in early manuals for confessors, as a guide to the solution of difficult cases after they had occurred. But a casuistical formation in moral theology tended to make confessors and directors of conscience consider these minimal and extraordinary cases almost as if they were ordinary norms. It is one thing to assert*

that in an extreme and exceptional situation a "lesser evil" may be "permitted" (though not "directly willed") and quite another to build a whole theory of Christian ethics on boundary line cases where the exceptional and the minimal becomes the norm.[8]

Meanwhile primary Christian values, Merton argued, have been left in ruins:

What hope is there of genuinely Christian conduct if it is assumed a priori as quite normal to regard the death of an innocent child as a "lesser evil" than one's own capture? What happens, in such circumstances, to the Christian emphasis in the Gospel and in the early Church, on the sacrifice of one's own interests for others? What, in a word, happens to the Christian emphasis on the greater good? It is replied that such emphasis is "only of counsel" and is "not demanded."[9]

In *Peace in the Post-Christian Era*, Merton did not reject the just war doctrine, but pointed out, as he had in the essay "Target Equals City," how even wars that have manifestly just causes tend gradually to adopt methods that undermine the war's moral legitimacy:

When a war has been begun as a "just war," it may turn into an unjust war when clearly unjust means are resorted to and when the inhumanity of unlimited ruthlessness takes possession of the combatants and strategists. There is no denying that in the heat of war, the morality of the "just war" doctrine tends to be forgotten. This has been particularly true in modern warfare which has become more and more aggressive and offensive, and in which the overwhelming power of aerial bombardment has been unleashed against the enemies' cities and civilian populations.... In World War II, in which the Allied forces fighting Nazism undoubtedly had a just cause ... [but] the ruthless policy of demanding "unconditional surrender" led to greater and greater fury in their use of air bombardment and culminated in the atomic destruction of Hiroshima and Nagasaki.... The slaughter of civilians [in both Germany and Japan] was explicitly intended as

---

8. In the chapter "The Legacy of Machiavelli" (PPCE, 52-53).

9. Ibid., 53.

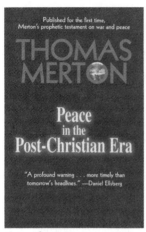

Cover for *Peace in the Post-Christian Era*

a means to "breaking enemy morale" and thus breaking his "will to resist." This was pure terrorism[10]

Repeatedly Merton discussed the problem of obedience in carrying out manifestly immoral actions:

The history of Nazi Germany shows us how appalling was the irresponsibility which would carry out even the most revolting of crimes under the cover of "obedience" to "legitimately constituted authority" for the sake of a "good." This moral passivity is the most terrible danger of our time.[11]

Have we forgotten that for the Nazis the greatest virtue, the greatest reasonableness, was to be found in blind obedience to the destructive mania of the Fuehrer?[12]

Merton went on to make the case for Christian disobedience when obedience would be sinful:

Now let us suppose that the political leaders of the world, supported by the mass media in their various countries, and carried on by a tidal wave of greater and greater war preparations, see themselves swept inexorably into a war of cataclysmic proportions. Let us suppose that it becomes morally certain that these leaders are helpless to arrest the blind force of the process that has irresponsibly been set in motion. What then? Are the masses of the world, including you and me, to resign [ourselves] to our fate and march to global suicide without resistance, simply bowing our heads and obeying our leaders as showing us the "will of God"? I think it should be evident to everyone that this

---

10. In the chapter "Justice in Modern War" (PPCE, 58-59).
11. In the chapter "Moral Passivity and Demonic Activism" (PPCE, 12).
12. In the chapter "Red or Dead: The Anatomy of a Cliché" (PPCE, 126).

can no longer, in the present situation, be accepted unequivocally as Christian obedience and civic duty.[13]

In a chapter on the formation of Christian conscience Merton noted that the key issue is not political or ideological:

The real problem of our time is basically spiritual. One important aspect of this problem is the fact that in many Christians, the Christian conscience seems to function only as a rudimentary vestigial faculty, robbed of its full vigor and incapable of attaining its real purpose: a life completely transformed in Christ.... Genuine Christian action has .... to be based on a complete sacrificial offering of our self and our life, in the service of truth. Short of this, we cannot attain sufficient detachment from our own selfish interests and from the peripheral concerns of a wealthy, spiritually indolent society. Without this detachment we cannot possibly see nuclear war as it really is, and we will consequently betray Christ and His Church, in the mistaken conviction that in defending our wealth we are defending Christian truth.[14]

Merton singled out Dorothy Day as someone providing an example of a life shaped by a well-formed Christian conscience that inspired not only her hospitality to the down-and-out but her occasional acts of peaceful civil disobedience:

There are many reasons to believe that the social action of someone like Dorothy Day, who is willing to refuse cooperation even in civil defense drills and ready to go to jail for her belief in peace, is far more significantly Christian than the rather subtle and comfy positions of certain [theologians]. When I consider that Dorothy Day was confined to a jail [after choosing to sit on a park bench in front of City Hall rather than go into a designated bomb shelter] in nothing but a light wrap (her clothes having been taken from her) and that she could only get to Mass and Communion in the prison by dressing in clothes borrowed

---

13. In the chapter "The Christian Choice" (PPCE, 155-56).

14. In the chapter "Christian Conscience and National Defense" (PPCE, 149, 150-51).

from prostitutes and thieves in the neighboring cells, then I lose all inclination to take seriously the self-complacent nonsense of those who consider her kind of pacifism sentimental.[15]

For a book written more than half a century ago, inevitably parts of *Peace in the Post-Christian Era* appear dated, yet the major elements of Merton's analysis remain all too timely. In many ways the world is little different from what it was in 1962. Then as now, one need not have an overactive imagination to envision Doomsday. Death by nuclear explosion is only one of many grim futures we can all too easily imagine for ourselves. The possible use by terrorist groups of radioactive material or even of nuclear weapons casts a dark shadow over anyone's ideas about the future.

The continuing unwillingness of the United States to fully engage in such international bodies as the International Court of Justice unless doing so suits its national interests would not surprise Merton. As he wrote in *Peace in the Post-Christian Era*:

Indeed the big powers have been content to use the United Nations as a forum for political and propagandist wrestling matches and have not hesitated to take independent action that led to the discrediting of the UN whenever this has been profitable to them.[16]

The same mind-set is linked to the readiness to initiate preemptive war "based not on the fact that we ourselves are actually under military attack, but that we are 'provoked' and so 'threatened' that even the most drastic measures are justified."[17]

Merton would not be surprised that Americans still take it for granted that evil is committed by it enemies, not themselves, hence the widespread bewilderment that so good-willed a people are the object of so much enmity:

Faced by the supercilious contempt of friends as well as the hatred of our avowed enemies, and wondering what there is in us to hate, we

---

15. Ibid., 151.
16. In the chapter, "Can We Choose Peace?" (PPCE, 21).
17. In the chapter "Working for Peace" (PPCE, 90).

have considered ourselves and found ourselves quite decent, harmless and easygoing people who only ask to be left alone to make money and have a good time.[18]

Among the positive changes that have occurred since Merton wrote *Peace in the Post-Christian Era* is that among Christians the words "peace" and "peacemaking" are no longer the suspect terms they were in 1962, a change in attitude that is partly owing to Merton. An outstanding example is the May 1983 pastoral letter of the U.S. Catholic Bishops, "The Challenge of Peace: God's Promise and Our Response." In a Merton-like voice, the pastoral letter broke new ground by incorporating the principle and strategy of nonviolence into Catholic social teaching:

The Christian has no choice but to defend peace, properly understood, against aggression. This is an inalienable obligation. It is the how of defending peace which offers moral options. . . . We see many deeply sincere individuals who, far from being indifferent or apathetic to world evils, believe strongly in conscience that they are best defending true peace by refusing to bear arms. In some cases they are motivated by their understanding of the Gospel and the life and death of Jesus as forbidding all violence. In others, their motivation is simply to give personal example of Christian forbearance as a positive, constructive approach toward loving reconciliation with enemies. In still other cases, they propose or engage in "active nonviolence" as programmed resistance to thwart aggression, or to render ineffective any oppression attempted by force of arms. No government, and certainly no Christian, may simply assume that such individuals are mere pawns of conspiratorial forces or guilty of cowardice (ch. 73).[19]

The Catholic Church has become a more outspoken advocate of peace since Merton's time. Its commitment to seek peace has not wilted despite such events as the terrorist attacks of September 11,

18. In the chapter "Working for Peace" (PPCE, 18).

19. www.usccb.org.

2001, or America's subsequent "preemptive" war in Iraq, or its military actions to promote "regime change" in other countries.

A striking sign of the times is the fact that several years ago the Archdiocese of New York proposed that Dorothy Day be formally recognized as a saint and placed on the calendar of the Catholic Church. The Vatican has already given her the title "Servant of God." In September 2015, Pope Francis identified her as one of four Americans he especially admires.

Were he alive and well and no longer hobbled by censorship, perhaps Merton would set to work on updating *Peace in the Post-Christian Era*. Many paragraphs, even chapters, could remain unaltered or very similar. No doubt he would remind us once again that Christ waves no flags and that Christianity belongs to no political power bloc. Once again he would affirm that "an essential part of the 'good news' is that nonviolent and reasonable measures are stronger than weapons. Indeed, by spiritual arms, the early Church conquered the entire Roman world."[20]

---

20. In the chapter "Beyond East and West" (PPCE, 96).

Cold War Letters

THE BRITISH NOVELIST EVELYN WAUGH once teased Merton with the suggestion that, so fine were his letters, Merton should give up writing books and concentrate on communication that required only postage stamps.[1] The command that stopped Merton from writing for the general public about war and peace issues effectively forced him to take up Waugh's advice, at least when writing about topics regarded by his abbot general as inappropriate for a Trappist monk. The five-volume set of Merton's letters, the bulk of them written in the last decade of his life, provides an overview, on a person-by-person basis, of what the uncensored Merton had to say on a wide range of topics.[2]

Those with whom Merton corresponded included a number of people who were, in one way or another, engaged in efforts to prevent war and to promote nonviolent alternatives to military conflict, among them Dorothy Day, Dan and Philip Berrigan, Jim Douglass, Jean and Hildegard Goss-Mayr, Gordon Zahn, W. H. Ferry, John Heidbrink, June Yungblut, Tom Cornell, and myself. He was a prolific correspondent. In my own case, between 1961 and 1968, I received more than seventy letters from him plus many postcards and notes as well as several telegrams.

---

1. In *The Sign of Jonas*, Merton wrote: "Evelyn Waugh ... thought it would be a good idea for me simply to put books aside and write serious letters, and make an art of it" (SJ, 126). For a detailed account of their relationship, see Mary Frances Coady, *Merton and Waugh: A Monk, A Crusty Old Man, and The Seven Storey Mountain* (Brewster, MA: Paraclete Press, 2015).

2. The five volumes were published by Farrar, Straus and Giroux. There is also a one-volume collection of some of Merton's most notable letters, *Thomas Merton: A Life in Letters* (TMLL).

In the latter part of 1961, wanting to share with a wider circle some of the letters he was sending to individuals, Merton came up with the idea of editing a self-published collection of his *Cold War Letters*,[3] as he christened them, for distribution to friends and friends of friends. As with the monastery's under-the-radar edition of *Peace in the Post-Christian Era*, Dom James Fox gave his blessing to the project, and a younger monk was assigned to type stencils and run off a mimeographed edition.

Cold War Letters, with "strictly confidential—not for publication" on the title page, appeared in two editions. In the first there were forty-nine letters written between October 1961 and March 1962; in the second printing, an additional sixty-one letters were added, the last of them dated October 30, 1962. Altogether there were a hundred and eleven letters that had been posted to eighty-one persons. In addition to social activists, the recipients included fellow monks, nuns, priests, bishops, artists, poets, writers, theologians, a nuclear physicist, and people in or close to the political establishment. In the last category was Ethel Kennedy, wife of Attorney General Robert Kennedy and sister-in-law of President John Kennedy. Ethel Kennedy had initiated a correspondence with Merton in the summer of 1961.

The thirteen-month span reflected in *Cold War Letters*, Monsignor William Shannon has observed, was "the most vigorous, concentrated and productive period of Merton's writings on war and peace."[4]

Altogether an estimated six hundred copies of the spiral-bound book were produced and given away. How many readers *Cold War Letters* had at the time is impossible to know, but they must have numbered in the thousands. Each copy was a message in a bottle thrown into the waves by a monastic castaway.

The letters not only addressed the arms race, the Cold War, the realities of nuclear war, and the temptations to launch a preemptive

---

3. A trade edition of *Cold War Letters* was published by Orbis Books in 2006.
4. *Cold War Letters* (CWL), 20.

nuclear strike on the Soviet Union, but they also touched on a wide range of other matters of interest to Merton. Though each of the letters had some degree of Cold War content, the book provided the readers with a 360-degree view of Merton as he was at the time, a Merton free of the barricades of censorship, a Merton of far-ranging interests. Nor did he whitewash his tribulations with the Trappists. Even his "Low Sunday" epistle to me, with his outraged reflections on being silenced, was included. With *Cold War Letters*, Merton was broadcasting his abbot general's gagging order far and wide.

"In *Cold War Letters* we encounter Thomas Merton at his very best, written to us at our collective worst," comments theologian Jim Douglass in his introduction to the Orbis edition of the book. "Never before, perhaps, has a contemplative seen the darkness more clearly, nor been more powerless to act on what he saw. In these letters to a circle of correspondents that encompassed the world, [Merton's] perception and anticipation of the [October 1962 Cuban] Missile Crisis is startling.[5] He is not only a prophet, in the most demanding sense of the word, but a totally fearless explorer of the Cold War psyche. He plunges our warring heads into the cold waters of our fearful selves."[6]

In her preface to the Orbis edition of *Cold War Letters*, Christine Bochen notes that "Merton's position against war and for peace is rooted in a thoughtful and critical consideration of two radically different ways of viewing the world and of living in it. One way is

---

5. The Cuban Missile Crisis was a thirteen-day confrontation between the United States and the Soviet Union over Soviet nuclear-armed missiles that had been deployed in Cuba. It played out on television worldwide and was the closest the Cold War intentionally came to nuclear war. In response to the Bay of Pigs Invasion of April 1961 and the presence of American inter-continental ballistic missiles in Italy and Turkey that placed Moscow in range, Soviet leader Nikita Khrushchev agreed to Cuba's request to place nuclear missiles in Cuba in order to deter any future attack on Cuba. In the end the Soviet missiles were withdrawn from Cuba and American missiles from Italy and Turkey. For a detailed account, see "October Missile Crisis" on Wikipedia.

6. CWL, xvi.

Cover for *Cold War Letters*

informed by a 'Cold War mentality,' the other by Christian humanism."[7]

The first, Bochen explains, is rooted in an oversimplified view that divides the world into two camps, with America on the side of heaven and total evil on the other side. Thus, in Merton's words, "everything the enemy does is diabolical and everything we do is angelic. His H-bombs are from hell and ours are the instruments of divine justice. It follows then that we have a divinely given mission to destroy this hellish monster and any steps we take to do so are innocent and even holy."[8]

In contrast with the two-dimensional, bumper-sticker mentality of the cold warrior, Bochen finds, was Merton's Christian humanism. Such a Christ-centered humanism was, in Merton's words, "rooted in the Incarnation ... [and] in the biblical notions of man as the object of divine mercy, and of special concern on the part of God, as the spouse of God, as, in some mysterious sense, an epiphany of the divine wisdom."[9] For Merton the Christian humanist sees the other, including his enemy, not merely as a convenient or inconvenient object but as another self, "no less deserving of the divine mercy than I am."

Many of the letters gathered into the book were marked by a sense of desperate urgency. For Merton, as he put it in the first of the *Cold War Letters*, launching a nuclear war "would be purely and simply the crucifixion over again."[10]

"At present," he told Archbishop Thomas Roberts, "my feeling is that the most urgent thing is to say what has to be said and say it

---

7. CWL, xxvii-xxx.
8. CWL, 5.
9. CWL, 22.
10. CWL, 10.

in any possible way. If it cannot be printed, then let it be mimeo-graphed. If it cannot be mimeographed, then let it be written on the backs of envelopes, as long as it gets said."[11]

Might Merton have been too extreme in his anxieties? Not at all, it turns out. Only in recent years, with the declassification of docu-ments that were once top secret, has it become known, to give one example, that on July 20, 1961, several months before Merton's first Cold War letter was written, the Pentagon's Joint Chiefs of Staff and the National Security Council presented President Kennedy with a plan for a surprise nuclear attack on the Soviet Union that would occur, if the president approved the plan, late in 1963.[12] To his ever-lasting credit, Kennedy walked out of the meeting in disgust. "And we call ourselves the human race," he afterward said to Secretary of State Dean Rusk.[13]

One of the questions that remains unanswered is whether any of the letters Merton sent to Ethel Kennedy were shared by her with President Kennedy, though certainly Merton was aware of that pos-sibility. In a letter sent to Ethel in December 1961, Merton seems to be standing in the Oval Office and might have prefaced his text with the words "Mister President":

> It seems to me that the great problem we face is not Russia but war itself. War is the main enemy and we are not going to fully make sense unless we see that. Unless we fight [against] war, both in ourselves and in the Russians, ... we are purely and simply going to be wrecked by the forces that are in us.... We [Americans] have made mistakes and will make more of them, but I hope we can learn to be a bit more realistic about all that, as long as we avoid the biggest mistake of all: plunging the world into nuclear war by any deliberate decision of our own.... It is tremendously important for us to work out a collabora-tive control scheme with the USSR to check on various possible acci-dents that might trigger a nuclear war....

---

11. CWL, 26.

12. See James Galbraith, "Did the US Military Plan a Nuclear First Strike for 1963?"; http://prospect.org/article/did-us-military-plan-nuclear-first-strike-1963.

13. See Dean Rusk's memoir, *As I Saw It* (New York: Norton, 1990), 246-47.

> *It seems to me that there are very dangerous ambiguities about our democracy in its actual present condition. I wonder to what extent our ideals are now a front for organized selfishness and systematic irresponsibility. The shelter business certainly brought out the fact that some Americans are not too far from the law of the jungle. If our affluent society ever breaks down and the façade is taken away, what are we going to have left? Suppose we do have a war, and fifty million people are left to tell the tale: what kind of people are they going to be? What kind of a life will they live? By what standards? We cannot go on living every man for himself....* [14]

A recurrent theme in Merton's writings in this period was his pained awareness of how many Americans, including Catholics both lay and clerical, advocated or passively supported a unilateral nuclear attack on the Soviet Union, regarding it as a "lesser evil," the assumption being that if the United States waited too long, the Soviet Union would launch its own first strike.

Alert to major lapses in moral leadership in recent times, Merton repeatedly referred to the failure of the Catholic Church in Germany to declare that Hitler's expansionist wars blatantly failed to meet the criteria of the just war doctrine. On the contrary, German and Austrian Catholics were solemnly called upon by their bishops to take part in these wars, while the rare conscientious objectors, such as Franz Jägerstätter, were counseled to take the military oath and went to their executions unsupported by their church.

"Jägerstätter is to me a moving symbol of a lonely isolated Christian who was faithful to his conscience, in the supremely difficult question of the most real and the highest kind of obedience,"[15] Merton commented in a letter to Gordon Zahn, author of *German Catholics and Hitler's Wars* and of a biography of Jägerstätter, *In Solitary Witness.*[16]

---

14. CWL, 27.

15. CWL, 50.

16. It is noteworthy that, while supporting Hitler's wars, a number of bishops and many priests objected to various aspects of Nazism: racism, anti-Semitism, neo-paganism, and euthanasia. Bishop Clement August van Galen of Munster

As happened in Germany, said Merton in another letter, American Christianity has become a "Christianity of passive conformity, in which, under the name of obedience, we are often brought into subjection to the most worldly influences and powers."[17]

Merton saw Nazi Germany's concentration camps, in which millions perished, as prefiguring nuclear holocaust. "The whole Christian notion of man has been turned inside out," Merton wrote to Bruno Schlesinger, a correspondent in Indiana. "Instead of paradise we have Auschwitz."[18]

In both *Peace in the Post-Christian Era* and *Cold War Letters*, Merton cited declarations of recent popes condemning war and the targeting of cities. Even before Hiroshima, in 1944 Pius XII had declared that "the theory of war as an apt and proportionate means of solving international conflicts is now out of date." What was most notable about such statements for Merton was how little interest American Catholic bishops took in making papal teaching on war widely known. In contrast, Catholic opposition to abortion and birth control, the topic of countless sermons and pastoral letters, was known to even the most nonattentive occasional Mass attender. In a letter to Oxford scholar Etta Gullick, Merton commented wryly:

> One would certainly wish that the Catholic position on nuclear war was held as strictly as the Catholic position on birth control. It seems a little strange that we are so wildly exercised about the "murder" (and the word is of course correct) of an unborn infant by abortion, or even the prevention of conception, which is hardly murder, and yet accept without a qualm the extermination of millions of helpless and innocent adults, some of whom may be Christians and even our friends rather than our enemies. I submit that we ought to fulfill the one without omitting the other.[19]

---

described the church in Germany as an anvil being beaten by the Nazi hammer, but added, "The anvil usually outlives the hammer."

17. CWL, 64.

18. CWL, 22.

19. CWL, 38.

A Christian is obliged to be aware of political and military realities of the time he or she lives in—to read the signs of the times—but is even more obliged to be anchored in the deep waters of an active spiritual life. Otherwise a change of heart and the formation of an active, healthy conscience is impossible. As Merton wrote me soon after my first visit at the monastery, a letter subsequently included in *Cold War Letters*:

> *My Mass on February 1st, the Feast of St. Ignatius Martyr of Antioch, will be for . . . all who yearn for a true peace, all who are willing to shoulder the great burden of patiently working, praying, and sacrificing themselves for peace. We will never see the results in our time, even if we manage to get through the next five years without being incinerated. What we have known in the past as Christian penance is not a deep enough concept if it does not comprehend the special problems and dangers of the present age. Hairshirts will not do the trick, though there is no harm in mortifying the flesh. But vastly more important is the complete change of heart and the totally new outlook on the world of man. We have to see our duty to mankind as a whole. We must not fail in this duty which God is imposing on us with His own hand.*[20]

For Merton a change of heart was essential before nonviolent methods could be recognized as a practical alternative to violence and war. As he wrote to Charles Thompson, a leader of the Pax Society in England:

> *The great issues that face us are the defense of man, the defense of truth, the defense of justice. But the problems in which we are immersed spring from the fact that the majority of men have a totally inadequate and rudimentary idea of what can constitute an effective "defense of man." Hence the transparent absurdity of a situation in which mass societies soberly and seriously prepare to defend man by wiping him out. Our first task is to liberate ourselves from the assumptions and prejudices which vitiate our thinking on these fundamental*

---

20. CWL, 59.

points, and we must help other men to do the same. This involves not only clear thought, lucid speech, but very positive social action. And since we believe that the only really effective means are nonviolent, we must learn nonviolence and practice it. This involves in its turn a deep spiritual purification.[21]

In *Cold War Letters* there are repeated references to Gandhi. Both Gandhi and Martin Luther King, Jr., had shown that nonviolence not only provided an effective strategy of protest but also contributed to profound social change in ways that were unobtainable by violent means. (When Merton was in his teens he had taken an interest in Gandhi and his nonviolent campaign to end British imperial rule of India. That interest was greatly revived during the last decade of his life. In 1965 New Directions published an anthology, *Gandhi on Nonviolence*, edited and with an introduction by Merton.)

Genuine nonviolence for Merton had to be more than a negative state of demonstrating without violence. Protest may be superficially nonviolent and yet communicate contempt for one's adversaries and bring out the worst in them. In one of the *Cold War Letters*, Merton wrote about this problem, addressing me as someone involved in public protest:

One of the most problematical questions about nonviolence is the inevitable involvement of hidden aggressions and provocations. I think this is especially true when there are a fair proportion of non-religious elements, or religious elements that are not spiritually developed. It is an enormously subtle question, but we have to consider the fact that in its provocative aspect, nonviolence may tend to harden the opposition and confirm people in their righteous blindness. It may even in some cases separate men out and drive them in the other direction, away from us and away from peace. This of course may be (as it was with the prophets) part of God's plan. A clear separation of antagonists. And perhaps now we have to see that this may be all we can do: simply clarify the issue.

---

21. CWL, 184.

Gandhi (GandhiServe)

Anyway we can always direct our action towards opening people's eyes to the truth, and if they are blinded, we must try to be sure we did nothing specifically to blind them. Yet there is that danger: the danger one observes subtly in tight groups like families and monastic communities, where the martyr for the right sometimes thrives on making his persecutors terribly and visibly wrong. He can drive them in desperation to be wrong, to seek refuge in the wrong, to seek refuge in violence.

The violent man is, by our standards, weak and sick. Though to us at times he is powerful and menacing in an extreme degree. In our acceptance of vulnerability, however, we play on his guilt. There is no finer torment. This is one of the enormous problems of the time, and the place. It is the overwhelming problem of America: all this guilt and nothing to do about it except finally to explode and blow it all out in hatreds, race hatreds, political hatreds, war hatreds. We, the righteous, are dangerous people in such a situation. (Of course we are not righteous, we are conscious of our guilt above all, we are sinners: but nevertheless we are bound to take courses of action that are professionally righteous and we have committed ourselves to that course.)

This is not for you so much as for myself. We have got to be aware of the awful sharpness of truth when it is used as a weapon, and since it can be the deadliest weapon, we must take care that we don't kill more than falsehood with it. In fact, we must be careful how we "use" truth, for we are ideally the instruments of truth and not the other way round.[22]

Along similar lines, another letter to me included in *Cold War Letters* stressed the importance of compassion toward those who are outraged by acts of protest:

Of course the tragedy is that the vast majority of people do not understand the meaning of this kind of witness. In their pitiful blind craving for undisturbed security they feel that agitation for peace is somehow threatening to them. They do not feel at all threatened by the bomb, for some reason, but they feel terribly threatened by some little girl student carrying a placard, or by some poor workingman striking in protest. Somehow they feel that it is after all possible for people to change their mind and revise their whole attitude towards a setup that has its enormous disadvantages but—at least it is "what we are used to, and please God don't ask us to get used to something else." Unfortunately the bomb is going to impose a terrible adjustment on those who may be left around to adjust. And it is with this that people want

---

22. CWL, 69-70.

to defend themselves. We have to have deep patient compassion for the fears of men, for the fears and irrational mania of those who hate us or condemn us.[23]

Among the factors that blind us to the divine image in the other, especially the enemy, and turn society toward violence is, in Merton's view, our entrapment in the "magic" of technology. In a letter to author and diplomat Claire Boothe Luce, Merton stressed the problem of out-of-control technology:

Our sudden, unbalanced top-heavy rush into technological mastery has left us without the spiritual means to face our problems. Or rather, we have thrown the spiritual means away. Even the religious people have not been aware of the situation, not become aware until perhaps too late. And here we all stand as prisoners of our own scientific virtuosity, ruled by immense power that we ought to be ruling and cannot. Our weapons dictate what we are to do. They force us into awful corners. They give us our living, they sustain our economy, they bolster up our politicians, they sell our mass media, in short we live by them. But if they continue to rule us we will also most surely die by them. For they have now made it plain that they are the friends of the "preemptive strike." They are most advantageous to those who use them first. And consequently nobody wants to be too late in using them second. Hence the weapons keep us in a state of fury and desperation, with our fingers poised over the button and our eyes glued to the radar screen.[24]

The word "pacifism" figured in a number of the *Cold War Letters*. In the sense that Merton had personally renounced killing anyone, a stand he had first formally declared in a letter to his draft board in 1941 and which he never abandoned, Merton was certainly a pacifist. Yet in a number of letters as well as in *Peace in the Post-Christian Era,* he denied the pacifist label, insofar as it suggested he had renounced the church's just war doctrine or condemned those who were not conscientious objectors. Though he personally would not take part in any war, he could imagine wars of self-defense against

---

23. CWL, 58-59.
24. CWL, 43.

invaders that might meet the criteria of a just war. But if the conditions of a just war were taken seriously, no war could be considered just insofar as it targeted noncombatants or used weapons of mass destruction. As he put it to a correspondent in Kansas:

> *Though not a total pacifist in theory myself, I certainly believe that every Christian should try to practice nonviolence rather than violence and that some should bind themselves to follow only the way of peace as an example to the others. I myself as a monk do not believe it would be licit for me ever to kill another human being even in self-defense and I would certainly never attempt to do so. There are much greater and truer ways than this. Killing achieves nothing. Finally, though as I said in theory I would still admit some persons might licitly wage war to defend themselves (for instance the Hungarians [resisting Soviet troops] in 1956), yet I think that nuclear war is out of the question, it is beyond all doubt murder and sin. . . .*

In fact, Merton added, even small wars of self-defense were problematic:

> *Since in practice any small war is likely to lead to nuclear war, I therefore believe in practice that war must be absolutely banned and abolished today as a method of settling international disputes.*[25]

Merton never felt at home in arguments that sought to establish the ethical limits of violence, arguments—such as killing a neighbor in defense of one's fallout shelter—that impressed him for the absence of actual Christian content. He preferred the gospel, in which everything is centered on love of God and neighbor, with "neighbor" meaning whoever is standing in front of you, friend or foe. One of the collection's most memorable texts, part of a letter to Dorothy Day, was a reflection on love:

> *Persons are known not by the intellect alone, not by principles alone, but only by love. It is when we love the other, the enemy, that we obtain from God the key to an understanding of who he is, and who we are. It*

---

25. CWL, 14-15.

Women Strike for Peace protests during the Cuban
Missile Crisis. (Library of Congress)

*is only this realization that can open to us the real nature of our duty,
and of right action.*

*To shut out the person and to refuse to consider him as a person,
as an other self, we resort to the impersonal "law" and "nature." That
is to say we block off the reality of the other, we cut the intercommu-
nication of our nature and his nature, and we consider only our own
nature with its rights, its claims, its demands. And we justify the evil
we do to our brother because he is no longer a brother; he is merely an
adversary, an accused.*

*To restore communication, to see our oneness of nature with him,
and to respect his personal rights and his integrity, his worthiness of
love, we have to see ourselves as similarly accused along with him, condemned to death along with him, sinking into the abyss with him, and*

needing, with him, the ineffable gift of grace and mercy to be saved. Then instead of pushing him down, trying to climb out by using his head as a stepping stone for ourselves, we help ourselves to rise by helping him to rise. When we extend our hand to the enemy who is sinking in the abyss, God reaches out for both of us, for it is He first of all who extends our hand to the enemy. It is He who "saves himself" in the enemy who makes use of us to recover the lost groat which is His image in our enemy.[26]

Circulation of *Cold War Letters* was one aspect of a significant widening of perception that had been underway in Merton for several years—a growing awareness that his contemplative vocation linked him not only with God but with the human race in its totality, and that God was calling him, as a writer with an immense audience, to raise his voice as best he could against the nuclear-equipped violence that now threatened everyone's life. Any writing about "the spiritual life" that ignored the threat of total war was a falsification of what it meant to be a follower of Christ. His efforts to write about the crisis via a book having been prevented, *Cold War Letters* opened a small but significant door. At the same time, for those who had access to the letters, Merton was not only revealing his views of war but was also unmasking himself more completely than had been permitted in his books. The letters also revealed Merton's dissent within his own monastic order. In the book's preface, he acknowledges that the letters are "biased by a frank hatred of power politics and by an uninhibited contempt for those who use power to distort truth or to silence it altogether."

---

26. CWL, 30-31.

Pacem in terris

WITH THE PUBLICATION OF Pope John XXIII's encyclical *Pacem in terris* (Peace on Earth) in April 1963, the silenced Merton found the pope himself saying to the entire world the kinds of things Merton had formerly been saying in the pages of *The Catholic Worker*. Pope John flatly declared that war could no longer be considered "a fit instrument with which to repair the violation of justice."

While the publication of papal encyclicals is normally of interest only to more committed Catholics, *Pacem in terris* proved to be a dramatic exception. Its release was front-page news, stirring up discussion and debate around the world. Many newspapers published extensive excerpts, while some published the full text. Before long major conferences centering on *Pacem in terris* were organized in many countries. Pope John was seen as having provided, as one commentator put it, "a bill of rights and obligations for the human race."

Such an unprecedented reception was due in part to this being the first encyclical addressed not only to Catholics but to "all people of good will." Here was a pope who, in the last months of his life, made an appeal for peace both to believer and atheist, and did so at a time when millions of people were aware that they would more likely die of nuclear war than of illness or old age. Published at a time when American military leaders were seriously considering a "first strike" attack on the Soviet Union, it is not unreasonable to say that Pope John's declaration helped prevent a cataclysmic third world war.

Pope John XXIII

The framework of the text was a listing of human rights and human duties.

88

The foundational human right, Pope John pointed out, is the right to life. Without that right, no other right has any meaning. As no human activity so undermines the right to life as war, peacemaking is among the highest and most urgent of human callings.

One of Pope John's major themes was conscience. "The world's Creator," he said in the opening section, "has stamped man's inmost being with an order revealed to man by his conscience; and his conscience insists on his preserving it." Quoting from St. Paul's letter to the church in Rome, he added, "Human beings 'show the work of the law written in their hearts. Their conscience bears witness to them'" (Rom. 2:15).

The pope went on to declare that conscience could not be coerced, either in religious matters or in the relationship of the person to the state:

> Hence a regime which governs solely or mainly by means of threats and intimidation or promises of reward, provides men with no effective incentive to work for the common good. Authority is before all else a moral force. For this reason the appeal of rulers should be to the individual conscience, to the duty which every man has of voluntarily contributing to the common good. But since all men are equal in natural dignity, no one has the capacity to force internal compliance on another. Only God can do that, for He alone scrutinizes and judges the secret counsels of the heart. Hence, representatives of the State have no power to bind men in conscience, unless their own authority is tied to God's authority, and is a participation in it (48-49).

In case the reader missed the implications, Pope John pointed out that laws that violate the moral order have no legitimacy and do not merit our obedience:

> Governmental authority ... is a postulate of the moral order and derives from God. Consequently, laws and decrees passed in contravention of the moral order, and hence of the divine will, can have no binding force in conscience, since "it is right to obey God rather than men." ... A law which is at variance with reason is to that extent unjust and has no longer the rationale of law. It is rather an act of

violence. . . . *Thus any government which refused to recognize human rights or acted in violation of them, would not only fail in its duty; its decrees would be wholly lacking in binding force* (51, 61).

The time is urgent, John noted:

[All of us are living] in the grip of constant fear, . . . afraid that at any moment the impending storm may break upon them with horrific violence. And they have good reasons for their fear, for there is certainly no lack of . . . weapons [of mass destruction]. While it is difficult to believe that anyone would dare to assume responsibility for initiating the appalling slaughter and destruction that [nuclear] war would bring in its wake, there is no denying that the conflagration could be started by some chance and unforeseen circumstance. . . . [T]he very testing of nuclear devices for war purposes can, if continued, lead to serious danger for various forms of life on earth. Hence justice, right reason, and the recognition of man's dignity cry out insistently for a cessation to the arms race. The stockpiles of armaments which have been built up in various countries must be reduced all round and simultaneously by the parties concerned. Nuclear weapons must be banned (111-12).

Pope John gave particular attention to dangers posed by weapons of mass destruction, declaring that, in this context, it is absurd to regard war as just:

Men nowadays are becoming more and more convinced that any disputes which may arise between nations must be resolved by negotiation and agreement, and not by recourse to arms. We acknowledge that this conviction owes its origin chiefly to the terrifying destructive force of modern weapons. It arises from fear of the ghastly and catastrophic consequences of their use. Thus, in this age which boasts of its atomic power, it no longer makes sense to maintain that war is a fit instrument with which to repair the violation of justice (126-27, emphasis added).

In June, two months after the publication of *Pacem in terris*, Merton wrote once again to the order's abbot general, Dom Gabriel

Sortais, in a fresh attempt to get the gagging order lifted. In a letter written to me a week later, he told me of this attempt:

> *I wrote to the Abbot General and said it is a good thing Pope John didn't have to get his encyclical [Pacem in terris] through our censors and could I now start up again. I will let you know what happens. The General is probably impregnable in his serene conviction that he really wants me to preserve the contemplative silence of our mystic order and that is his "only motive."*[1]

Specifically Merton asked if he might now return to work on *Peace in the Post-Christian Era* so that it might finally be published. His mind unchanged, Dom Gabriel renewed the prohibition. "I am not asking you to remain indifferent to the fate of the world," Dom Gabriel insisted. "But I believe you have the power to influence the world by your prayers and by your life withdrawn into God more than by your writings. That is why I am not thinking about hurting the cause you are defending when I ask that you give up your intention of publishing the book you have finished, and abstain from now on from writing on the subject of atomic warfare, preparation for war, etc." Merton commented in his journal, "At the back of [Dom Gabriel's] mind obviously is an adamant conviction that France [of which Dom Gabriel was a citizen] should have the bomb and use it if necessary. He says that the encyclical [*Pacem in terris*] has changed nothing in the right of a nation to arm itself with nuclear weapons for self-defense."[2]

Merton himself probably didn't realize that his own war–peace writings might have played a part in the drafting of *Pacem in terris*, but there was a significant bond between himself and John XXIII. Merton had begun writing to Pope John just two weeks after his

---

1. HGL, 274; letter dated April 26 1963. Merton's next effort to ease restrictions was made the next year following Dom Gabriel's death and the election of his successor. In a letter to me dated March 16, 1964, Merton wrote, "I am in trouble with the new General already. I wanted to republish in a book some of the peace articles that had been permitted in magazines.... He wants to prevent even republication of articles that were [previously] permitted [by the order's censors]" (HGL, 279).

2. TTW, May 10, 1963.

Papal stole, a gift of Pope John XXIII to Thomas Merton. (Photo by Jim Forest)

election in 1958. In a remarkable gesture made in April 1960, the pope had shown his personal respect and affection for Merton by sending him, in the care of a Venetian friend, one of his stoles, a liturgical vestment embroidered with symbols of the papal office.[3] Merton responded with a gift of his own for John, a copy of the hand-press edition of *What Ought I to Do?*, his translation of stories and sayings of the early desert monks.[4]

Writing to Pope John in November 1961, just weeks after publication of his first *Catholic Worker* article, Merton had spoken of the "grave threat" of nuclear war. The "lack of understanding, ignorance and violent and subtle propaganda ... conspire together to create a very unsettling mood in the United States" with the result that "many hate communist Russia with a hatred that implies the readiness to destroy that nation." War and preparation for war had now become so embedded in the economy that, for many people, disarmament would cause financial ruin. "Sad to say," Merton continued, "American Catholics are among the most war-like, intransigent and violent." Monsignor Loris Capovilla, John XXIII's private secretary, later noted that the pope was especially impressed by Merton's letter.[5]

---

3. The stole can be seen at the Thomas Merton Center at Bellarmine University in Louisville, Kentucky.

4. An expanded trade edition entitled *Wisdom of the Desert* (WD) was published by New Directions in 1965.

5. HGL, 486. Pope Francis named Capovilla a cardinal in 2014.

One of Merton's few post-silencing peace texts that managed to see the light of day under his own name was a statement written in response to the award in 1963 of the Pax Peace Prize, presented *in absentia* by Harvard University history professor H. Stuart Hughes.[6] After apologizing for his inability to come to Cambridge for the presentation, Merton went on:

> *A monastery is not a snail's shell, nor is religious faith a kind of spiritual fallout shelter into which one can plunge to escape the criminal realities of an apocalyptic age.*
>
> *Never has the total solidarity of all men, either in good or in evil, been so obvious and so unavoidable. I believe we live in a time in which one cannot help making decisions for or against man, for or against life, for or against justice, for or against truth.*
>
> *And according to my way of thinking, all these decisions rolled into one (for they are inseparable) amount to a decision for or against God.*
>
> *I have attempted to say this in the past as opportunity has permitted, and opportunity has not permitted as much as I would have liked. But one thing I must admit: to say these things seems to me to be only the plain duty of any reasonable being. Such an attitude implies no heroism, no extraordinary insight, no special moral qualities, and no unusual intelligence. . . .*[7]

He proceeded to offer brief quotations, "perfectly obvious and beyond dispute," from *Pacem in terris*, including Pope John's statement that "the arms race ought to cease, that nuclear weapons should be banned, that an effective program of gradual disarmament should be agreed upon by all nations."

> *[Such] propositions . . . are obvious, and clear as daylight. . . . If I said it before* Pacem in terris, *that still does not make me terribly original,*

---

6. For details about the award, see "Thomas Merton and the Pax Peace Prize," in *The Merton Seasonal* 33, no. 1 (Spring 2008): 3-14.

7. *The Nonviolent Alternative* (NVA), 257-58.

because the same things were said long ago by popes before Pope John, and by theologians, and by the Fathers of the Church, and by the Gospels themselves. . . .

I don't deserve a medal for affirming such obvious and common sense truths. But if by receiving the medal I can publicly declare these to be my convictions, then I most gladly and gratefully accept.

This same year that *Pacem in terris* was published, Merton wrote a preface for the Japanese edition of *The Seven Storey Mountain*. In it he drew the reader's attention to changes that had occurred in his attitudes and assumptions since writing the autobiography. While putting no direct stress on topics he had been forbidden to write about, he addressed them obliquely:

I have learned . . . to look back into the world with greater compassion, seeing those in it not as alien to myself, not as peculiar and deluded strangers, but as identified with myself. In freeing myself from their delusions and preoccupations I have identified myself, nonetheless, with their struggles and their blind, desperate hope of happiness.

But precisely because I am identified with them, I must refuse all the more definitively to make their delusions my own. I must refuse their ideology of matter, power, quantity, movement, activism and force. I reject this because I see it to be the source and expression of the spiritual hell which man has made of his world: the hell which has burst into flame in two total wars of incredible horror, the hell of spiritual emptiness and sub-human fury which has resulted in crimes like Auschwitz or Hiroshima. This I can and must reject with all the power of my being. This all sane men seek to reject. But the question is: how can one sincerely reject the effect if he continues to embrace the cause?

Merton went on to say that he had always regarded his conversion to Christ "as a radical liberation from the delusions and obsessions of modern man and his society," and that religious faith alone "can open the inner ground of man's being to the liberty of the sons of God, and preserve him from surrender of his integrity to the seductions of a totalitarian lie."

He spoke of his present understanding of the monastic life:

The monastery is not an "escape from the world." On the contrary, by being in the monastery I take my true part in all the struggles and sufferings of the world. To adopt a life that is essentially non-assertive, nonviolent, a life of humility and peace is in itself a statement of one's position. But each one in such a life can, by the personal modality of his decision, give his whole life a special orientation. It is my intention to make my entire life a rejection of, a protest against the crimes and injustices of war and political tyranny which threaten to destroy the whole race of man and the world with him. By my monastic life and vows I am saying No to all the concentration camps, the aerial bombardments, the staged political trials, the judicial murders, the racial injustices, the economic tyrannies, and the whole socio-economic apparatus which seems geared for nothing but global destruction in spite of all its fair words in favor of peace. I make monastic silence a protest against the lies of politicians, propagandists and agitators, and when I speak it is to deny that my faith and my Church can ever seriously be aligned with these forces of injustice and destruction.

He noted regretfully that others who believe in war also invoke the faith, just as they support racial injustices and engage in "self-righteous and lying forms of tyranny." He declared:

My life must, then, be a protest against these also, and perhaps against these most of all.

The problem for contemporary Christians, he continued, is to end the identification of Christianity with those forms of political society that dominate Europe and the West, just as was done by the early Christian monks in the fourth century in distancing themselves from a church that had become the object of imperial favor, membership in which meant career advancement:

The time has come for judgment to be passed on this history. I can rejoice in this fact, believing that the judgment will be the liberation of Christian faith from servitude to and involvement in the structures of the secular world. And that is why I think certain forms of Christian "optimism" are to be taken with reservation, in so far as they lack the genuine eschatological consciousness of the Christian vision, and concentrate upon the naive hope of merely temporal achievements—[such as building] churches on the moon!

If I say No to all these secular forces, I also say Yes to all that is good in the world and in man. I say Yes to all that is beautiful in nature, and in order that this may be the yes of a freedom and not of subjection, I must refuse to possess anything in the world purely as my own. I say yes to all the men and women who are my brothers and sisters in the world, but for the yes to be an assent of freedom and not of subjection, I must live so that no one of them may seem to belong to me, and that I may not belong to any of them. It is because I want to be more to them than a friend that I become, to all of them, a stranger.[8]

No longer allowed to write about war and obliged not to comment on nuclear weapons, ironically Merton wrote instead of the deep resistance that was needed in a world that had suicidal tendencies.

---

8. "Preface to the Japanese Edition," *The Seven Storey Mountain* (*Nanae No Yama*). The text is included in *"Honorable Reader": Reflections on My Work* (HR), 63-67.

Building a Catholic Peace Movement

"THE CATHOLICS IN THE PEACE MOVEMENT we are now starting,"
Merton told Eric Fromm in a letter sent in December 1961, "are not
the most influential in the country by any means, quite the contrary.
Some of us are [part] of an already notoriously pacifist group, the
Catholic Worker, tolerated by all as a sign that we can find a mansion
for beats in the church as well as for the respectable. There are a few
priests, no bishops."[1]

The "Catholic peace movement we are now starting" was at the
time less an existing group than a proposal that had been made not
many weeks earlier to Merton, me, and several other Catholic pacifists by John Heidbrink, Church Work secretary of the Fellowship
of Reconciliation. The FOR, in those days almost solidly Protestant
in staff and membership, was the oldest peace organization in the
United States, dating back to the beginning of World War I in 1914.[2]
One of the conditions for membership was the refusal to sanction or
participate in war in any form. A number of denominational peace
fellowships were associated with the FOR—Methodist, Episco-
pal, Presbyterian, Baptist, Lutheran, Unitarian, and others. Deeply
impressed by Pope John XXIII and the Catholic Worker's history of
war resistance, the thought had arisen in John Heidbrink's mind that
the time might be ripe to found a "Catholic Peace Fellowship." He
proposed that the CPF launch itself with the publication of a booklet containing Merton's *Catholic Worker* article, "The Root of War Is
Fear." The FOR would pay, he said, for the booklet's publication and

---

1. CWL, 15-16.
2. The Fellowship of Reconciliation in the United States was part of the International Fellowship of Reconciliation. Catholic participation in IFOR had been
substantial from its inception.

also cover the cost of mailing it out, along with a letter introducing CPF, to Catholic bishops, priests, nuns, and laypeople all over the country.

I read John's letter aloud over lunch to see how the idea struck the rest of the Catholic Worker staff. Dorothy's initial response was negative—"Those Protestants just want to use you," she said rather grumpily. But the next day she remembered things she liked about the FOR and could see that there was peace work to be done for which the Catholic Worker had neither the staff nor the resources. All we could do on our own was publish the paper and carry on the demanding work of maintaining a house of hospitality. We were ill equipped to counsel Catholic conscientious objectors, put competent speakers on the road, and do the sort of organizing work that was desperately needed if the Catholic community was to discover certain submerged elements in its own tradition, particularly as regards conscience, vocation, and peacemaking—the Gospel of the Beatitudes.

In November 1961 John Heidbrink and I met for an evening meal at Ratner's, a kosher dairy restaurant on Second Avenue whose waiters presided like doctors over their customers' diets. Nourished by borscht and blintzes, the Catholic Peace Fellowship had its first faint beginnings in a milieu as Jewish as a yeshiva in Jerusalem. Soon afterward I visited John and some of his colleagues at the FOR headquarters in Nyack, New York, and once there I signed up as a FOR member and agreed to set up a meeting to discuss the FOR proposal with others who might take an interest. I also wrote to Merton about what we were up to.

A meeting was quickly organized that convened at the Manhattan apartment of Eileen Egan, friend of Dorothy and a senior staff member of Catholic Relief Services. To my disappointment, it quickly became clear that a Catholic peace group linked to the mainly Protestant FOR would too easily be dismissed by most Catholic bishops and clergy—such was the anti-ecumenical climate that prevailed at the time. Half a century later it is hard to recall how massive and fortified from both sides was the wall of prejudice that divided Catholics and Protestants before the Second Vatican Council.

[H]AT TAKETH
[T]HE SWORD
[S]HALL PERISH
[B]Y THE SWORD
Jesus

Dorothy Day in protest for peace. (Courtesy Marquette University Library)

Recognizing the basic value of Heidbrink's proposal, however, participants in the meeting decided to establish an America sister group of the British Catholic peace association, the Pax Society.[3] At a subsequent meeting it was agreed that the U.S. Pax group would publish a journal and host an annual conference.

I wrote Merton to let him know how the group was developing. He immediately became a member of Pax and also agreed to be listed as a sponsor.

Partly on the advice of Merton, it was agreed that Pax, despite its Catholic Worker roots, would not describe itself as "pacifist" but instead use such expressions as "gospel peacemaking" and "gospel nonviolence."

"About the word 'pacifist,'" Merton commented in a letter to Eileen Egan. "This is really an important semantic problem which touches on theology and requires a little thought.... One of the urgent tasks of Pax is the education of Catholics on this point.... If by pacifist we mean 'peacemaker,' then a Catholic is obliged to be one." But, Merton continued, a problem with the word is that it has become understood in the English-speaking world "in the Protestant and liberal context of individualism," an approach that is problematic for most Catholics even though it is acceptable "insofar as the individual conscience is always to be respected." If the word is to be used, "we must make clear that it is to be understood ... not just as individual and subjective revulsion of war, but a Catholic protest, based on the mind of the church, against the use of war as a way of settling international disputes." Merton concluded with the advice

---

3. Eleven years later Pax became the U.S. branch of Pax Christi International.

that it would be best for Pax to avoid words that would marginalize it. "Until the word [pacifist] is thoroughly cleared of [negative associations] one must be rather circumspect in using it, but I would say that with a little care and patience it could be rehabilitated."[4]

In the meantime, while remaining part of Pax, I became active with a more secular peace group, the Committee for Nonviolent Action (CNVA), working at its office on Grand Street in Lower Manhattan. Founded in 1958, CNVA was one of the first peace groups to focus on creating imaginative, dramatic demonstrations on both land and sea that sought to heighten public awareness of the growing danger of nuclear war and promote disarmament. Gandhi provided much of the group's inspiration. Among CNVA's actions were protests at nuclear test sites and walks for peace, the longest of which was a 6,000-mile disarmament march from San Francisco to Moscow that I—still in the Navy at the time—had briefly joined when it passed through Washington, DC.

In the spring of 1962, CNVA's main project was sailing a boat christened *Everyman* into a restricted region of the South Pacific in which the United States intended to explode hydrogen bombs. Though the detonations were described as tests, in fact they were demonstrations of U.S. resolve to make use of such city- and region-destroying weapons if it decided to do so.[5] It was beyond irony that one of the bomb targets bore the name *Christmas* Island.

In a predawn letter dated May 17, 1962, Merton noted he was aware that the *Everyman* was setting sail that very day. He wrote that he had tacked a notice about it on the novices' bulletin board, had

---

4. See Eileen Egan, *Peace Be with You* (Maryknoll, NY: Orbis Books, 1999), 215-16.

5. Operation Dominic, as it was called, occurred during a period of intense Cold War tension between the United States and the Soviet Union. America's Bay of Pigs invasion of Cuba had occurred not long before. Soviet Premier Nikita Khrushchev announced the end of a three-year moratorium on nuclear testing on August 30, 1961, and Soviet tests recommenced on September 1. President John F. Kennedy responded by authorizing Operation Dominic, the largest nuclear weapons testing program ever conducted by the United States.

sent a telegram of support to the crew, and in three hours would be saying Mass for them, noting that it was "still early and dark and the birds are waking up." He found it ominous that the nuclear test was called "Operation Dominic" and wondered if so naming it had any connection with the Dominican Inquisition. "I think the courage and alertness manifested in the building and sailing of *Everyman* is significant in a high degree. The CNVA is alive as few organizations are." Yet Merton also voiced a note of caution: "[Such a] project is . . . an improvisation. You must be careful of that, because the temptation to multiply improvisations as if they were miracles may be dangerous to CNVA eventually. What is needed is that [Gandhi-like] ashram [community], and deep roots from which these things grow more slowly and firmly."[6]

A month later there was another letter. After congratulating me for joining the staff of Catholic Relief Services, Merton commented further on the *Everyman* project:

> *I was not surprised at what happened to Everyman. [The U.S. Coast Guard had stopped the boat and arrested the crew; they were subsequently jailed in Honolulu.] Although it seems to me the [U.S. government] action has no legal basis whatever, it is purely and simply an arbitrary act of power, because we are getting more and more into a situation where power has supplanted law, and the precise effect of a protest like Everyman is that it brings this out. . . .[7]*

A letter from Merton in August first commended me for getting significantly engaged with a local parish, Saint Theresa's, on the Lower East Side of Manhattan:

> *It is especially important for you to be working in and with the parish at the moment. The Church is after all a reality, though her members have failed shockingly in their Christian responsibility in many areas, and though there may be great blindness and weakness pervading whole areas of her life, nevertheless she is indefectible because God*

6. HGL, 268.
7. HGL, 268-69.

lives and acts in her. And this faith must live in us and grow in us, especially when we are tempted against it as we are now. I think you will get a great deal out of this effort.[8]

Perhaps sensing I was too uncritical of the peace movement in which I was so immersed, Merton went on to make some cautionary remarks. Groups like CNVA, he said, "have great potentiality, yet I think it remains terribly superficial. But then everything is superficial now." He saw himself as being in no position to provide any remedies, as he was unable to keep "a right perspective" despite letters and articles sent to him by me and other friends. "I am really out of the game and can't do much in the ordinary way."

Merton's next letter, dated September 22, brought the news that he had joined the Fellowship of Reconciliation—"a rather obvious thing to do." Meanwhile an expanded edition of *Cold War Letters* was being mimeographed; he promised to send me copies. He was pleased but also bewildered with the news I had sent him that the Committee for a Sane Nuclear Policy (SANE) was producing its own edition of *Peace in the Post-Christian Era*:

I had heard absolutely nothing about this and have no idea who gave them the book for this purpose. . . . On the other hand, I am never sure whether a letter came and never reached me. I have no objection . . . as long as they are discreet and don't get me into a jam with the authorities (Church) which could affect my other writings. I don't think there is anything whatever wrong with the book from the Church's official point of view, but if it raises a lot of discussion in the wrong place, among stupid people who complain to bishops, then it will inevitably get back to my superiors and they will want to know what's all this, who do I think I am, and I will be permanently shut up about everything except the rosary."[9]

In a letter dated November 7, Merton returned to the core theme of his banned peace writing:

8. HGL, 270.
9. HGL, 270-71.

[The challenge of war] is a most essential issue, one of the cardinal moral issues of our time, one on which the witness of the Church will depend, yet most American Catholics are failing in their response. Clear anti-war statements from the popes are ignored unless militarists can find clauses that give a loophole. . . . The real issue is then the recognition of the individual conscience to access the facts of the case, as well as the principle of the just war.[10]

A month later Merton commented on a CNVA project then underway to break the blockade the United States had imposed on Cuba by attempting to deliver urgently needed medical supplies via a boat similar to *Everyman*. Merton regarded the project as feasible and desirable, one that reached beneath the barricades of politics to reveal "the human dimension":

It seems to me that the basic problem is not political, it is apolitical and human. One of the most important things is to keep cutting deliberately through political lines and barriers and emphasizing the fact that these are largely fabrications and that there is another dimension, a genuine reality, totally opposed to the fictions of politics: the human dimension which politics pretends to arrogate entirely [to itself]. . . . This is the necessary first step along the long way . . . of purifying, humanizing and somehow illuminating politics themselves. Is this possible? . . . At least we must try. . . . Hence the desirability of manifestly non-political witness, non-aligned, non-labeled, fighting for the reality of man and his rights and needs . . . against all alignments.[11]

In his next letter Merton wrote that for nonviolent action to reach its transformative potential more than ideology is required:

[What is needed is] a more solid foundation, and deeper roots, spiritual roots. I know you have them already, but an immense amount of work needs to be done by us all. We have got to work on the theological and spiritual bases for ahimsa *[a Hindi word often used by Gandhi that means non-killing] and tie them in with the Gospel in a way that*

---

10. HGL, 272.
11. HGL, 272.

leaves no doubt as to the Christian obligation in this regard. As long as these deep foundations are not there, I think you can very well be used or misused by political elements that have nothing to do with you. . . .[12]

In a letter sent in March 1963 Merton stressed the importance of a conscientious objection that goes beyond refusal to participate in war:

Hence the importance of nonviolent people who are really conscientious objectors not only to nuclear war but to everything that leads to it or goes with it in the same general atmosphere of violence and criminality. The perspectives of the nonviolent movement have to be enlarged in all directions, so that it becomes a genuine and profound spiritual movement, and a force for life in a rotting and corrupt world.[13]

Looking for ways to escape to a greater degree the limitations imposed on him, in addition to distributing his peace writings to friends via mimeograph, Merton began publishing occasional articles using names other than his own. The June 1963 issue of *The Catholic Worker* included an essay on the remarkably successful and entirely nonviolent effort that Danes, under Nazi occupation, had made to save their Jewish population. The author was someone named Benedict Moore.[14] Another *Catholic Worker* article was by-lined by Benedict Monk. A letter to *Jubilee* magazine was signed Marco J. Frisbee.

The Marco J. Frisbee letter was in the satiric tradition of Jonathan Swift's "A Modest Proposal." Noting that many theologians were doing their best to demonstrate that nuclear war was "a brave and Christian thing after all," the Frisbee-masked Merton suggested that it was time to move beyond "the wishy-washy moralism of the Sermon the Mount" and instead revive human sacrifice:

---

12. HGL, 273.

13. HGL, 273; letter dated March 27, 1973.

14. "Danish Non-Violent Resistance to Hitler" (PFP, 150-53).

I think we ought to go back to the well-known practice of the Kings of Israel and Judah in the fifth and sixth centuries B.C. when they were having so much trouble with Assyria and Babylon. They too were disgusted by sentimentality and moralism, and they went right-directly into the heart of the problem with a genuine red blooded, religious rite: the sacrifice of the first born.

"I realize," Frisbee/Merton continued, "that this suggestion will shock sentimentalists, but this is no time to worry about their cringing susceptibilities." Besides reviving an ancient tradition that presumably pleased the gods of war, a number of secondary benefits were listed, including the reduction of the number of troublesome teenagers, though the author added it would perhaps be best to make the offering before the child is five "and thus easier to catch." Another plus: "Junior's brothers and sisters are going to get a new outlook on life assisting in this moving ceremony. It will give them an inkling of what it means to live in the modern world. . . ."[15]

---

15. Merton's "Marco J. Frisbee" letter was a response to an article published in *Jubilee* in January 1962. I received it from Merton in February. It was never published but is included in the appendix, see p. 192. In April I asked Merton for permission to make some mimeographed copies. He replied: "OK, on the feast of San Marco how could Marco Frisbee refuse? Print it and send me 2 dozen copies." (unpublished handwritten note dated April 25, 1962).

Founding the Catholic
Peace Fellowship

DURING THE TWO YEARS SINCE PAX was started, the idea of forming a Catholic Peace Fellowship had been put on hold but not abandoned. As 1964 began, with more and more U.S. troops being sent to Vietnam, the moment seemed at hand to finally launch CPF. The work of Pax was aimed mainly at organizing an annual conference and getting out an occasional journal, *Peace*—good work, but it seemed to me too timid. CPF could supplement what Pax was doing by concentrating on reaching ordinary people, including high school students and young adults who would become the cannon fodder of war if U.S. military involvement in Vietnam intensified. Wasn't it time to vigorously promote conscientious objection as an option for Catholics?

In February Merton wrote to say that starting such a fellowship sounded timely, so long as it did not duplicate efforts being made by Pax: "[But] I suppose Pax just isn't [very active at present]. I haven't had much contact with them at all and really have no idea what is going on there if anything. However ... there is something to be said for [launching CPF], and the fact of putting out good literature, study kits and so on will be very valuable."[1] Merton sent two packets of his abstract calligraphies to be exhibited—"at an espresso gallery," he suggested—and sold as a way of raising a little start-up money for the CPF.

CPF began taking shape that summer. John Heidbrink had received a donation from Hermene Evans, one of the few Catholic members of FOR, to pay for the costs of several Catholics to join in a two-week seminar in Europe that was to begin in France in mid-June and go on from there to Italy, Switzerland, and Czechoslovakia,

---

1. HGL, 279; letter dated February 27, 1964.

Calligraphy by Thomas Merton
(Thomas Merton Center, Bellarmine University)

where we would participate in an East-West "Christian Peace Conference."

Jesuit priest and poet Dan Berrigan, then on sabbatical in France, met us on arrival in Paris. A highlight of our three-day stay there was a meeting Dan had arranged with Jean Daniélou, fellow Jesuit priest and eminent scholar of the early church. Daniélou, later made a cardinal by Pope Paul VI, was one of the theological advisors—*periti*—for the Second Vatican Council. He spoke to us about theologians of the first centuries of the Christian era, such saints as Gregory of Nyssa and his brother Basil the Great, who, using the modern term, could be described as pacifists.

Jim Douglass, then doing doctoral work at the Gregorian University in Rome, became part of our group once we arrived at Leonardo da Vinci Airport. Among meetings Jim had arranged for us was one with curia member Augustin Bea, whom Pope John had made a cardinal in 1959 with the special task of heading the newly created Vatican Secretariat for the Promotion of Christian Unity. Bea, a German Jesuit and biblical scholar, was one of the bishops most closely linked with Pope John's aspirations for the Vatican Council. Welcoming our small group, he made clear how pleased he was to see Catholics and Protestants collaborating for peace. Responding to questions about the Vatican Council, he remarked on the divisions that existed among the bishops regarding the proposed condemnation of war fought with nuclear weapons and recognition of the right of refusal to condone or participate in war in any form—topics that were to be addressed in the council document on the church in the modern world, then known as Schema 13, still in the drafting stage. "There is resistance among some members of the American hierarchy to the Council taking a new direction in these matters," said Bea. The several Catholics at the meeting laughed at his polite understatement. "Your efforts are needed," Bea added, raising his hands and eyes toward heaven.

The following week we were in Prague. "Our stay here began bleakly," I wrote afterward to Merton, "but little by little a more hidden city revealed itself. We arrived, tired from traveling, having had little sleep and no time to unpack more than toothbrushes. Even the sun seemed gray. The Soviet-style hotel, built by forced labor we were told by our hosts, was unpleasant. But each day, quietly and in small ways, we discovered how wrong first impressions can be. Self-effacing Prague is a city of hidden virtues."

In his response Merton wrote: "I believe what you say about Prague. One of the most impressive Christians I have ever met is Jan Milic Lochman from the Comenius [theological faculty] there. He was here this spring. I got a card from him the other day. I feel I have much more in common with him than with many American Catholics."[2]

At the time Czechoslovakia was experiencing the "Prague Spring"—"socialism with a human face," was the widely used phrase. Our hosts proudly showed us a vacant pedestal on which a giant statue of Stalin once stood but lately had been removed. Unfortunately there were few parallel signs of a political spring in other parts of the Soviet Bloc. Four years later the Czech experiment would be crushed by Soviet tanks.

Much of the content of what was said by Eastern Europeans in

---

2. Unpublished letter to the author dated July 22, 1964.

front of conference microphones was embarrassingly similar to Soviet propaganda, but what we learned in informal conversations with Eastern participants made us more than ever aware of how close we were to nuclear war and how important it was to create doors and windows in the Iron Curtain. "We are Christians first," said one Czech theologian, "and bearers of a national identity only second. We are responsible for each other's lives. The pity is we have so little face-to-face contact. It is harder to kill people you know by name."

The resolution to cooperate in creating the Catholic Peace Fellowship became a covenant when the Catholics in the group were eating our evening meal in the medieval cellar of a restaurant in Prague. Gathered at one end of a long table, we talked about what CPF's focus should be and what we had to do to make that work possible. Our main goals were to organize Catholic opposition to the Vietnam War and launch a campaign to make known the fact that conscientious objection to war was an option not only for members of specifically pacifist "peace churches" but for Catholics as well. We also envisioned setting up a speakers' bureau and developing study kits for use in schools, universities, and seminaries. The only problem was that we had no staff, no office, and no money.

In mid-July I was back in America. Tom Cornell, my close friend and a former managing editor of *The Catholic Worker*, quickly became a partner in the work of laying the CPF's foundations. Together we drafted a statement of purpose and rented a post office box. Marty Corbin, the current *Catholic Worker* managing editor, became CPF co-chairman along with Fr. Philip Berrigan, a Josephite priest as well as Dan's brother. Phil had become a brave presence in the civil rights movement. Merton, while mentioning his increasing discomfort at being "a name," agreed to be on the CPF's board of sponsors, as did Dorothy Day, Dan Berrigan, and Archbishop Thomas Roberts.[3] With the help of friends, Merton among them, an address

---

3. Other sponsors included Baron Antoine Allard, Leslie Dewart, Jim Douglass, Father William DuBay, Hermene Evans, Edward Gargen, John Howard Griffin, Dom Bede Griffiths, Father Robert Hovda, Edward Keating, Robert Lax, Justus George Lawler, Father Robert McDole, Father Peter Riga, Karl Stern, Anton Wallich-Clifford, and Gordon Zahn.

list began to take shape. Rooted as it was in the Catholic Worker movement, the CPF took an unequivocally pacifist stand, emphasizing in its membership brochure the sweeping rejections of war made by popes John and Paul. A printer friend, Igal Roodenko of the War Resisters League, volunteered to design and print an initial run of five hundred sheets of CPF stationery. Igal's font collection included American Uncial, a typeface designed by Merton's friend Victor Hammer and inspired by medieval monastic script—perfect for the words "Catholic Peace Fellowship."

For the time being, whatever was to be done by CPF had to be done in my spare time. By now I was working as a reporter on the night shift of *The Staten Island Advance*, a daily newspaper. Between profiles of local citizens, news reports, social items, and obituaries, I often found an hour or two for CPF correspondence plus my own writing. My main spare-time project was an article for *The Catholic Worker* on the background of the war in Vietnam. The research was challenging. I was dismayed to discover how little about Vietnam was readily available even in the New York Public Library. For most Americans Vietnam was *terra incognita*—I doubt one out of a hundred of my neighbors could have found Vietnam on a world map even if rewarded with a twenty-dollar bill. Sending a copy of my completed Vietnam paper to Merton, I commented that "it should have been written at least a year ago—in fact we should have been on the rooftops protesting a year ago—but here we are fighting a fire blindfolded."

Responding to my draft, Merton commented that the situation in Vietnam "is completely poisonous. In a way it makes me much more disgusted and depressed than the [nuclear] tests ... because here the folly of it is spelled out ... in so much more human detail. ... [T]he whole thing stinks to heaven. ..."[4] In his previous letter Merton had remarked that he did not think the emerging war in Vietnam met any of the requirements to be regarded as just. "Because a few people in America want power and wealth, a lot of Vietnamese ... and Americans have been and will be sacrificed."[5]

---

4. Unpublished letter to the author dated July 22, 1964.
5. HGL, 281-2.

Early protest of the Vietnam War. Tom Cornell
holds a sign, with Jim Forest to the left of
Cornell. (Courtesy Tom Cornell)

By November the letters being delivered each week in the CPF
post box had grown from a trickle to more than the box could hold.
An office with a street address was a pressing need. Tom found that
the War Resisters League had two adjacent rooms, one currently
vacant, the other soon to be available. The location was excellent—at
5 Beekman Street, a block east of City Hall in lower Manhattan. Rent
was $25 a month per room, "our special rate for Catholic pacifists,"
said WRL office manager Ralph Digia. Taking a leap of faith that
was buoyed by a thousand-dollar donation from Hermene Evans,
we paid a hundred dollars in advance for the first four months and
signed up for a phone. Leaving my job with *The Advance* behind, on
New Year's Day 1965 Tom and I moved a desk, two chairs, and a file
cabinet into one of the rooms and put up a hand-lettered sign on the
door that read CATHOLIC PEACE FELLOWSHIP. Three months later
promises of financial support from several of the sponsors made it
possible for Tom to pull away from substitute teaching and become
fulltime CPF co-secretary.

The Spiritual Roots of Protest

READERS OF MERTON'S JOURNALS will quickly notice that Merton-the-monk had a complex, at times contentious, relationship with Merton-the-writer. In 1964, as leaves began turning red, yellow, and brown in Kentucky, Merton wondered if perhaps he had now said all that he needed to say about war and peace and that the time had come to slip quietly away from all controversies. Thus when I asked if he could be listed as a member of the Catholic Peace Fellowship's board of sponsors, he had said yes, but with hesitation. A response he sent me in early October gives the impression Merton was thinking aloud as he wrote, in a state of uncertainty and discomfort:

> I want to help, so I suppose you might as well use my name for the Peace Fellowship along with the others if it is of any use. The only thing is my feeling that it is a sort of useless gesture. Sure it is what is done, and it helps. But I think this is the last time [I will offer the use of my name in such a way]. It is true that if one has that illusory thing, "a name," it might as well be used for its illusion value. And yet I don't know if that really makes sense either. Anyway, I think this had better be the last illusion of this particular kind. But go ahead and put my name on the list.[1]

He had been thinking lately, he went on, about his efforts to speak out and "participate in some way in the noises of the public conscience," but found involvement in the fray too ambiguous. Were he to say less, he speculated, "it will not bother me or anyone else so much." In any event, Merton added, there were now people like Dan and Phil Berrigan to fill the gap.

---

1. HGL, 282.

Like so many earlier decisions to write less in order to inhabit a deeper silence, his resolution was abandoned almost immediately, in this case in part due to a preexisting commitment—Merton was hosting a retreat on peacemaking.

In late November, six weeks before the CPF was to have an office and, in myself, a full-time staff person, a small group of CPF- and FOR-related individuals arrived at the monastery for a three-day retreat to consider "the spiritual roots of protest," a topic worked out by Merton with the FOR's John Heidbrink.[2]

In a letter to Dan Berrigan, Merton had envisioned the retreat as unstructured: "Let's make it purposeless and freewheeling and a vacation for all, and let the Holy Spirit suggest anything that needs to be suggested."[3] In a letter to John Heidbrink, he wrote, "The great thing we can all try to do is get to those spiritual roots. My part is to offer whatever the silence can give." He proposed the retreatants attend the monastic offices of sung prayer as "Gregorian [chant] is good and it heals."[4]

My memories of the retreat begin with place and weather. The monastery was mainly made up of weathered, ramshackle buildings, with the oldest dating back more than a hundred years. The rolling hills of rural Kentucky were wrapped around the abbey on every side. The wind brought an occasional whiff of bourbon from distilleries in nearby Bardstown. The air was damp and chilly, the sky mainly overcast, with occasional rain.

It was due to the wet weather that there were only two sessions at Merton's hermitage, a small flat-roofed, one-story structure made of gray cinder blocks about a mile from the monastery. Perhaps to give the theme of the retreat a silent symbol, Merton had placed upturned, weathered roots from several trees on the porch of his hermitage. Our other meetings were in a room in the gatehouse normally used by families visiting monks. Whether in gatehouse or

---

2. For a carefully researched, hour-by-hour account of the retreat, see Gordon Oyer, *Pursuing the Spiritual Roots of Protest* (Eugene, OR: Cascade Books, 2014).

3. Merton to Berrigan, August 4, 1964 (HGL, 83-84).

4. Merton to Heidbrink, September 19, 1964 (HGL, 416).

Merton's desk in the hermitage. (Photo Thomas Merton,
courtesy Thomas Merton Center)

hermitage, it was a squeeze fitting all fourteen of us into the available space. Merton, wearing black-and-white Trappist robes, served as the retreat's central but never dominant figure. At each four-hour session one of the participants made a presentation about an hour long, at the end of which there was free-wheeling discussion.

This was my second meeting with Merton in person. Once again there was laughter, but less of it. The times were deadly serious—the near nuclear war over Cuba and the assassination of President Kennedy were still fresh memories—and so was much of the conversation. Merton spoke in earnest, listened with a quick and critical ear, and was more a fellow retreatant than the person in charge. As he prepared to speak to the group, I remember him pacing back and forth in front of his hermitage in a state of absorption so complete and compelling that it brought home to me the gravity of what he was going to say more than the words themselves.

One of the remarkable aspects of the retreat was that not all those taking part were Catholic, a fact that is unsurprising today but was almost unheard of in 1964. The most senior retreat participant was 79-year-old A. J. Muste, a Quaker who had once been a minister of the Dutch Reformed Church. A former executive secretary of the Fellowship of Reconciliation, he was now chairman of the Committee for Nonviolent Action. By the time of our gathering he was perhaps the most distinguished leader of the U.S. peace movement. There was John Howard Yoder, a Mennonite scholar; eight years later he would publish *The Politics of Jesus*, a book still widely read. W. H. Ferry, vice president of the Center for the Study of Democratic Institutions in California, was a Unitarian at the time who, later in life, described himself simply as a Christian. Elbert Jean was a Methodist minister from Nashville, Tennessee, who was deeply immersed in the civil rights movement. Nearly as venerable as A. J. Muste was Presbyterian John Oliver Nelson, a Yale professor who was a leader of the Fellowship of Reconciliation. Tony Walsh, a friend of Dan Berrigan, was founder of a Catholic Worker-like house of hospitality in Montreal named for Benedict Labré, a ragged saint who had lived a life of continual pilgrimage. John Peter Grady, another friend of Dan, was at the time business manager of *Jubilee*, the Catholic monthly magazine with which Merton was closely associated. Bob Cunnane was a Boston priest whose friendship with Phil Berrigan had begun through his brother, a classmate of Phil's at Holy Cross College. Cunnane's work included developing dialogue between Protestants and Catholics, Christians and Jews. Also present was another priest, Charles Ring, who worked closely with Cunnane in Boston. Finally there were Dan and Phil Berrigan, Tom Cornell, and myself. In the end, John Heidbrink, the retreat's co-architect, was unable to attend due to back surgery. Nearly everyone in the group was an FOR member; nine of the fourteen were Catholic, most of them involved in launching the CPF. That the group was made up entirely of men reflected the male tilt that still marked even groups working for radical social change, and Christianity as well. It wouldn't be until 1989 that renovations of the monastery guesthouse provided accommodation for women. Thus among those missing from the retreat was Dorothy Day.

Domine ut videam (Lord, that I might see). These three words, from Jerome's Latin translation of Mark's Gospel, are the appeal that Bartimaeus made to Jesus to open his blind eyes. This urgent prayer, used by Merton the first day, was at the heart of our retreat. Peacemaking begins with seeing, seeing what is really going on around us, seeing ourselves in relation to the world we are part of, seeing our lives in the light of the kingdom of God, seeing those who suffer, and seeing the image of God not only in friends but in enemies. What we see and what we fail to see defines who we are and how we live our lives. The day-by-day challenge is to be aware of the divine presence in the other, struggling not to be blinded by fear.

The theme of seeing was made all the more real by the presence among us of A. J. Muste. Shortly before his flight to Kentucky, A. J. had undergone successful surgery to remove cataracts from both eyes. At the Abbey of Gethsemani, A. J. was in a constant state of amazement. No leaf or flash of color went unappreciated. I have never seen anyone look at the world around him more attentively, so full of awe and gratitude. He helped all of us open our eyes a little wider.

Then there was another Latin phrase that Merton used: *Quo warranto*? (By what right?). In the context of the retreat this became, "By what right do we protest?" It wasn't a question I had ever before considered. I was born into a family in which protest was a normal activity— protest against injustice, protest against war, protest against racism, protest against cruelty. While not by nature a person drawn to protest, as a young

Cross in front of the hermitage.
(Photo by Jim Forest)

adult I found myself seeing protest as an unfortunate necessity. I could not watch preparations for war and fail to raise an opposing voice or refuse to participate in actions of protest and resistance. To protest was an unpleasant duty, period.

In raising the "by what right" question, Merton forced us to consider that protest, if it is to have any hope of constructive impact on others, has to be undertaken not only with great care but with a genuine sympathy and compassion for those who don't understand or who object to one's protest, who feel threatened and angered by it, who even regard the protester as a traitor. After all, what protest at its best aims at is not just to make a dissenting noise but to help others think freshly about our social order and the direction we are going. The protester needs to remember that no one is converted by anger, self-righteousness, contempt, or hatred. One has to use the hammer of protest carefully. Protest can backfire, harden people in their opposition, bring out the worst in the other. Sometimes this may be necessary—consider the confrontations that occurred in Selma just a few months earlier in which police and others brutally attacked nonviolent demonstrators simply wanting to exercise their constitutional right to vote. If it is to be transformative, protest needs to be animated by love, not love in the sentimental sense but in the sober biblical sense of the word. Hence Christ's insistence on love of enemies. "Until we love our enemies," Merton said, "we're not yet Christians."

"The grace to protest," Merton wrote in his notes for the retreat, "is a special gift of God requiring fidelity and purity of heart." Far from seeing an opponent merely as an obstacle, one wishes for him or her "a better situation in which oppression no longer exists."[5] Ideally, protest aims at change that benefits everyone.

Merton saw monasticism, in its origins, as a protest movement, and the early generations of monks as escapees from a world in which becoming a Christian, far from being the path to martyrdom, was an excellent career choice. Like sailors abandoning a sinking ship, the

---

5. Oyer, *Pursuing the Spiritual Roots*, 240.

Daniel Berrigan and Thomas Merton.
(Photo by Jim Forest)

pioneers of monasticism fled to the desert fringes rather than be part of a newly Christianized mainstream society.[6] Even today, in Merton's view, a monk—however unconsciously—is a person of protest, refusing a life of economic gain, refusing to be a consumer, refusing war. Every monk lives a life of deep nonviolence. A genuine monk, Merton said, is cloistered not by monastic architecture or by special clothing but by a cloistered heart. He gave as an example Saint John Gaulbert who, before becoming a Benedictine, forgave the man whom he had intended to kill, the murderer of his brother, instead throwing his sword into the river and embracing his would-be victim.

One of the issues Merton raised was how untroubled most Christians were by the militarization of American life and the blurring

---

6. This is a subject Merton developed in greater detail in his introduction to *The Wisdom of the Desert: Some Sayings of the Desert Fathers* (WD) (New York: New Directions, 1960).

together of national and religious identity. Summoned to war, few say no or even imagine saying no. Merton saw this as a problem not only in America but wherever nationalism is the primary shaper of one's identity. Merton spoke of "Kierkegaardian Christianity," the pseudo Christianity described by Kierkegaard in which the individual abdicates "conscience, personal decision, choice and responsibility," yielding himself to "pure myth."

By way of contrast, Merton reminded us of the life of Franz Jägerstätter, a name familiar to several of the retreatants but generally unknown at the time. Jägerstätter was an Austrian Catholic farmer, husband, father, and church sexton who, for his refusal to serve in the army of the Third Reich, was beheaded in Berlin on August 9, 1943. Despite his modest education, Jägerstätter had seen with amazing clarity what was going on around him, spoken out clearly and without fear to both neighbors and strangers about the hell Hitler's movement was creating, and finally—ignoring the advice of his bishop to take the military oath—paid for his obedience to conscience with his life.

Why, Merton asked, does Christianity produce so many who fight in manifestly unjust wars and so few, like Jägerstätter, who say no? "If the Church," said Merton, "could make its teachings alive to the laity, future Franz Jägerstätters would no longer give their witness in solitude but would be the Church as a whole reasserting the primacy of the spiritual."[7] (Little by little Franz Jägerstätter has come to be widely known. His story was to play a part in shaping what the Second Vatican Council had to say about conscience, conscientious objection, the limits of obedience, and, under some circumstances, the duty of disobedience. In 2007, during the pontificate of Benedict XVI, Jägerstätter was beatified at the cathedral in Linz, Austria. Blessed Franz is today recognized as a patron saint of conscientious objectors.)

_____

7. An essay on Franz Jägerstätter, "An Enemy of the State," is included in Merton's *Faith and Violence* (FV), 69-75. For further reading on the life of Jägerstätter, see Gordon Zahn, *In Solitary Witness* (1st ed.; New York: Holt, Rinehart and Winston, 1964; rev. ed.; Springfield, IL: Templegate, 1986); and *Franz Jägerstätter: Letters and Writings from Prison*, ed. Erna Putz (Maryknoll, NY: Orbis Books, 2009).

In a talk given on the second day, Dan Berrigan returned to the witness of Franz Jägerstätter and the questions raised by his life, emphasizing Jägerstätter's pained awareness that Christians were willing to yield virtually anything the Nazi regime demanded of them. Such a pattern of church surrender to political demands, Berrigan noted, wasn't new to the Hitler period nor unfamiliar in the postwar period—churches tend to preach and act within borders drawn by the state.

Austrian conscientious objector and martyr Franz Jägerstätter.

"Our only rightness is in our humility," Muste commented. "We must begin with the conclusion: 'There is no way to peace, peace is the way.'"[8] Developing the theme, Merton added, "Humility is vital in dealing with dissent. Who is the 'I' who [like Jägerstätter] can say 'no' to something? Don't think it's a matter of me versus society. In the broader world, the principalities have a corner on reality, and I must overcome the identity they project on me. Inadequate counter-efficacy is not the problem."[9]

In the handout Merton had given each of us at the beginning of the retreat, he had raised the question whether the technological

8. This much-quoted sentence is often attributed to Muste but was his only by adoption. In the summer of 1947, while visiting Le Chambon-sur-Lignon, a French village that rescued many Jews during the war, Muste heard Dr. Maurice Schwartz, a co-worker of André and Magda Trocmé, speak about the "two resistances." The first—"There is no way to God, God is the way"—summed up "the most important truth about religion." The second—"There is no way to peace, peace is the way"—revealed the harmony that exists between means and ends. Muste told the story in the December 1976 issue of *Fellowship*, journal of the Fellowship of Reconciliation.

9. Oyer, *Pursuing the Spiritual Roots*, 138, 145.

society "is by its very nature oriented to self-destruction or whether it can . . . be regarded as a source of hope for a new 'sacral' order . . . in which God will be manifested?"[10] One of the major elements of the retreat was taking a fresh look at ways in which technology so fascinates us that we become its prisoners. On the one hand technology solves many problems—Merton was grateful for the cleverly designed Coleman lantern that illumined his hermitage. On the other hand, military technology can destroy whole cities in a blinding flash while incinerating millions of people.

"*Domine ut videam*—Lord, that I might see." Again there is the problem of sight. We as a species have great difficulty seeing ahead—seeing the difference between the constructive and the destructive, though we know that a weapon, once made, is sooner or later likely to be used, and when that happens mainly innocent people will die.

In our discussion of technology one sentence in particular stands out in my memory: "If it *can* be done it *must* be done." Once a technological possibility is envisioned, no matter what dangers it poses, we seem as irresistibly drawn to making that vision real as Pandora was drawn to opening the box in which a legion of evil spirits were imprisoned. In the context of technology, in its almost monastically sheltered laboratories, the human being has come to be seen chiefly either as a consumer or as a "bio-chemical link"—in the latter case a necessary but unreliable bridge between the conscience-free, solid-circuit perfection of cyber systems.

Providentially the first copies of Merton's latest book, *Seeds of Destruction*, arrived during the second day of the retreat. The just-delivered box was brought to Merton in the room where we were meeting. Opening the package in the presence of his guests, Merton found there were enough copies for each retreatant to take one home, complete with an inscription from Merton. He explained that the book represented a partial breakthrough in his ongoing battle with Trappist censorship, as it contained what Merton saw as "the real heart of the forbidden book" [*Peace in the Post-Christian Era*] as

10. Ibid., 244.

(Photo by Jim Forest)

well as an essay on Gandhi and a selection of his *Cold War Letters*.[11]

Our three days together ended too quickly. Many questions had been raised, few if any resolved, but I'm certain all of us were haunted by the conversations we had taken part in. Perhaps Merton's main contribution was to impress on us the timeliness of holy disobedience such as Franz Jägerstätter exemplified—a costly nonviolent protest that reaches beyond slogans to the deepest roots of one's faith. It was in part thanks to the retreat that, in the years that followed, the Catholic Peace Fellowship did so much to promote awareness of the Jägerstätter story as a modern gospel parable.

---

11. DWL, 127.

Burning Draft Cards, Burning Bodies

SIX WEEKS LATER, and still invigorated by the retreat in Kentucky, the Catholic Peace Fellowship began a more intense phase of its work, opening a small office in lower Manhattan. The first of January 1965 can be regarded as the CPF's birthday.

Finances were precarious. Sixty-five dollars a week had been budgeted for salaries for Tom Cornell and myself, but weeks went by when there wasn't enough in the CPF bank account for me to write Tom's check or for Tom to write mine. In July, Dan and Phil Berrigan came to our homes for a meeting (we were living in adjacent apartments in the same building on Ridge Street on the Lower East Side). During deliberations about the poor state of CPF income, Phil discreetly looked into my refrigerator and Dan into the Cornells'. "In toto," Tom recalls, "they found two quarts of milk, a block of Velveeta cheese, and two half loaves of bread. Dan wrote a check. We were in business again."

The first significant CPF project was the publication of a brochure on conscientious objection, a double-sided single sheet of cream-colored paper, three columns to a side, folded to fit in a business envelope. Answering the question "Can a Catholic be a conscientious objector?" the text highlighted quotations on war and conscience from Pope John's *Pacem in terris*.[1] With the Vietnam War rapidly expanding with the full implementation of ground troops, starting in July 1965, and thousands of young men being drafted, the folder was in great demand; eight-thousand copies were distributed in the course of CPF's first eleven months.

---

1. Statements on war and conscience would become remarkable elements in *The Constitution on the Church in the Modern World*, but at the time that text was still being debated at the Second Vatican Council.

Tom Cornell and Jim Forest in the office of the Catholic
Peace Fellowship. (Courtesy Tom Cornell)

Before long we were counseling Catholic conscientious objectors
in droves—as many as fifty people a week phoned or wrote for help
or came to see us at the CPF office. Tom and I, later joined by Father
Lyle Young, spent many hours a week doing draft counseling.

A typical session of face-to-face or voice-to-voice draft counseling involved rehearsing questions a conscientious objector was
likely to be asked when he was summoned to defend his convictions
before his draft board and helping prepare the CO to answer them.
It wouldn't be easy. Few if any draft board members were likely to
be sympathetic. One question certain to be asked was: "In what circumstances, if any, have you made your views about conscientious
objection known to others?" The CO's initial response was often
an embarrassed silence followed by "None that I can think of." The
counselor would then ask, "You never talked to your parents about
this?" "Well, yes, there was that—lots of times." "It never came up
in conversations at school." "A lot!" "Did you take part in any anti-
war demonstrations." "Sure." Little by little the young war objector

realized he had done a great deal to make his views known. Other questions were likely to include: "How come other Catholics your age have no problem with military service? What makes you so different?" (Here it was essential to have some grounding in church teaching on war and conscience.) "What about World War II? Aren't you glad the Nazis didn't win?" (An answer might be, "I don't know what I would have done. All I know about are the kinds of wars being fought today.") And there was bound to be a question along these lines: "What you would do if your girlfriend was being raped?" ("Defend her, of course, but not kill the rapist. There are alternatives between passivity and murder.")

As Tom and I went out on speaking tours, CPF chapters began taking root in half a dozen cities, from Boston to San Francisco. A number of Catholic theologians and many clergy gave support, signed statements, arranged lectures, and joined in antiwar demonstrations.

As the war "escalated" (this was the odd verb used at the time by both the White House and the press), pressure increased on its opponents not to limit ourselves to educational programs but also to engage in acts of civil disobedience likely to result in jail time. Burning draft cards as an act of dissent became common enough for Congress, on August 29, 1965, to enact a law declaring the intentional burning or mutilation of draft cards a felony. President Lyndon Johnson signed that bill into law the very next day. Thus a minor symbolic act was made a prisonable offense. Two months later, David Miller, a young member of the Catholic Worker staff, decided it was time to part company with his draft card. At a rally in front of Manhattan's military induction center, David—after apologizing for not being a public speaker—set his card on fire. It was his wordless way of declaring he was willing to go to prison rather than be a soldier in Vietnam. And to prison he eventually went, sentenced to serve thirty months.

Three weeks later, on November 6, Tom Cornell plus four friends (David McReynolds of the War Resisters League, James Wilson, another Catholic Worker, Roy Lisker, and Marc Edelman) decided to replicate David Miller's action with the intention of arguing in court that such a gesture was a form of free speech, thus protected by the Constitution. Tom also reasoned the new law was a form of idolatry, treating as sacred a scrap of paper that in reality was simply an easily replicated government form of no intrinsic value.

The event took place on a stage at the north end of Union Square with a thousand people watching, including a small group of outraged counter-protesters who chanted, "Burn yourselves, not your draft cards." Dorothy Day and A. J. Muste spoke in support of the action, claiming co-responsibility. "I speak as one who is old," Dorothy said, "to endorse the courage of the young who themselves are willing to give up their freedom. I speak as one whose whole lifetime has seen the cruelty and hysteria of war. I wish to place myself beside A. J. Muste to show my solidarity of purpose with these young men and point out that we, too, are breaking the law, committing civil disobedience."

In his statement, Tom outlined the failure of protests that fell short of civil disobedience to bring politicians to seek peace:

> *Protests against the United States involvement in the war in Vietnam have been carried out with increasing intensity in recent months, dramatically disproving President Johnson's claim for consensus for his foreign policy. Still the war continues to escalate. Each day innocent peasants are being burned to death with napalm, their crops destroyed and their hopes dashed. American men are giving their lives. American families are being shattered to pursue a war that cannot be won, a war it was shameful of us to enter, a war we must all use our moral energy to halt so that we might set about building the conditions of peace.*
>
> *Americans have written to their congressmen. They have marched upon our nation's capital. They have paraded down Fifth Avenue. As conscientious objectors they have refused to serve in the armed forces. They have demanded that our nation address itself to the real problems that beset critical areas. Yet the war in Vietnam rages on and the seeds of war continue to proliferate and grow in Latin America and elsewhere.*

To intimidate and stifle the expression of protest and dissent, Congress passed a bill—*without debate*—making it a criminal offense to burn one's draft card, providing a five-year prison penalty and a $10,000 fine. On August 30, President Johnson signed that bill into law.

In the words of Karl Meyer of the Catholic Worker in Chicago, explaining to his draft board why he destroyed his card: "If the penalty for burning a paper card is so harsh, then the possession of the card becomes the universal act of fealty—incense on the altar of Caesar."

The grave crime, we are told, is not the destruction of life but the destruction of a piece of paper.

Peacemaker A. J. Muste with Dorothy Day at protest in Union Square. (Courtesy Marquette University Archives)

We cannot let this draconian law stand. Not only is the penalty provided outrageously disproportionate, but the very concept of the law indicates that the United States government, albeit accidentally and in a moment of frenzy, has taken upon itself the power to consecrate a piece of paper, invest it with a quality it cannot have, and then exact obeisance for that piece of paper. I can no longer carry that card.

For a number of reasons, I am not eligible for the draft. I am thirty-one years old, married and the father of a young son. Selective Service *examiners would not accept me. I could let the Vietnam War pass me by. But I feel that I must associate myself with David Miller, Steven Smith, and Karl Meyer in the open act of destroying my draft card, not in a spirit of defiance of public authority, but as a plea to my government and my fellow citizens to turn away from the present course in Vietnam, to turn away from intimidation and the stifling of dissent and protest at home, and to call upon like-minded people to stand with David Miller and the others who have expressed so forcefully their dedication to the cause of Peace on Earth.*

Many people have asked me how I can expose myself to such severe legal penalties when I have a wife and child to support. I can answer only in this way. Fellow Americans, sincere and conscientious soldiers, leave their wives and families to go to Vietnam, at the risk of their lives. We who have dedicated ourselves to the war against war, to the development of nonviolence as an effective means to resist tyranny, cannot shrink from accepting the consequences of our conscientious acts. My family and I have faith that God will provide for us as long as we attempt to do His will.

Tom Cornell and four others burn their draft cards in
Union Square. A. J. Muste looks on.
(Courtesy Tom Cornell)

Each of the five made a statement, then set their cards ablaze with a Zippo cigarette lighter. War opponents cheered, war supporters jeered. Police made a corridor through the crowd and guided the five to a patrol car. "As the car pulled away," Tom recalls, "one cop said 'Now you're safe!' Apparently the police knew there had been a threat of violence—this explained why there had been so many of them."

Simple though it was, the event attracted substantial national and even international attention. Eventually four of the five, Tom among them, were tried, found guilty, and sentenced to federal prison for six months.

Draft-card burning? Merton was one of the many people initially bewildered by the radical and provocative character of the action. In a letter to Tom he saw it as interfering with CPF's educational program and worried that the destruction of draft cards might alienate the very Catholics that the CPF was attempting to reach "with its apostolic work."[2]

Although Merton later reconsidered his criticisms of draft-card destruction, his fear that such forms of protests might have negative results became all too real three days later when, before dawn on the November 9, Roger LaPorte, a young Catholic Worker volunteer and former Cistercian novice, burned not his draft card but himself. Roger walked uptown to the U.S. Mission to the United Nations, doused himself with gasoline and set himself on fire. There was no written statement, but in an ambulance on the way to the hospital he managed to say: "I am against war, all wars. I did this as a religious action." He may have taken as his model Thich Quang Duc, a Vietnamese Buddhist monk who, two years earlier, had immolated himself on the streets of Saigon.

Too distressed to speak with journalists, Dorothy Day asked CPF to speak on her behalf. Her hope and ours was that Roger's action would not inspire others to do the same. For days, Tom and I were on the phone or writing statements from early morning till late at night.

---

2. Unpublished letter from Merton to Tom Cornell, December 5, 1965 (CPF 19/1, University of Notre Dame Archives).

Roger's self-immolation hit Merton like a bolt of lightning. On November 11, 1965, we received a telegram at the CPF office:

JUST HEARD ABOUT SUICIDE OF ROGER LAPORTE WHILE I DO NOT HOLD CATHOLIC PEACE FELLOWSHIP RESPONSIBLE FOR THIS TRAGEDY CURRENT DEVELOP-MENTS IN PEACE MOVEMENT MAKE IT IMPOSSIBLE FOR ME TO CONTINUE AS SPONSOR OF FELLOWSHIP PLEASE REMOVE MY NAME FROM LIST OF SPONSORS LETTER FOLLOWS THOMAS MERTON

We were ourselves still in a state of shock, struggling to absorb and understand Roger's horrific action. He would die later that day. Merton's telegram intensified our exhaustion and anguish.

Two days later, the thirteenth, the envelope we were expecting from Merton was delivered:

This is a bitter letter to have to write. This morning, after receiving the news of the suicide of Roger LaPorte, which I heard of quite by chance, I had to send you a telegram asking to remove my name from the list of sponsors of the CPF. I know of course that the CPF is not encouraging people to burn themselves up. Unfortunately, however, the CPF is in the middle of a peace movement in which ... there is something that looks to me to be a little pathological.

As you know, I am not sufficiently well informed to make clear judgments of this or that policy, for instance the burning of draft cards. Certainly protest is called for, and it may very well be that this precise form of protest is what is called for at the moment. I do not know. Maybe I am wrong in thinking that it is harming the peace movement rather

Dorothy Day, supporting draft card burners in Union Square. (Courtesy Marquette University Archives) *than helping it, and that it is in fact fanning up the war fever rather than abating it. . . .*

It seems to me that there is something radically wrong somewhere, something that is un-Christian, though I am not questioning anybody's sincerity and good will, or even the objective rights and wrongs of the clearest cases. But the whole thing gives off a very different smell from the Gandhian movement, the nonviolent movement in France and the nonviolence of Martin Luther King. Jim, there is something wrong here. I think there is something demonic at work in it. This suicide of a Catholic ex-seminarian (I was told) does not make sense in terms of a Christian peace movement. . . .

The spirit of this country at the present moment is to me terribly disturbing. To you too, and to everyone, no doubt. It is not quite like Nazi Germany, certainly not like Soviet Russia, it is like nothing on earth I ever heard of before. This whole atmosphere is crazy, not just the peace movement, everybody. There is in it such an air of absurdity and moral void, even where conscience and morality are invoked (as they are by everyone). The joint is going into a slow frenzy. The country is nuts.

For people to avail themselves of their right to conscientious objection which the [Vatican] Council has, thank God, finally acknowledged: that is what ought to be done. Instead, this business of burning oneself alive. What in heaven's name is the idea of that? It will only neutralize all the work that has been done and all the gains that have been made. What on earth are the American bishops going to make out of that? . . .

This morning I offered Mass for the peace movement and I shall certainly keep it in my prayers, particularly you and everyone associated with you. God bless you, and forgive me this hard letter.[3]

In my response to Merton's letter, while sympathizing with his sense that "the whole country is nuts," I argued the situation wasn't quite that bleak: "I do not mean to suggest we are in great shape . . . but there is much in the society that I think is healthy, growing

---

3. HGL, 285-87.

and good. Pro-war Vietnam arguments are not being swallowed whole. . . . At the core of what is sane in our society I think you will find the pacifist movement, constantly reminding the populace that life is sacred, that justice—not vengeance—is our job. . . . If this isn't sane, I don't know what is." I proposed that responsibility for Roger's death lay "not with a pathological peace movement but with a pathological reality, a fratricidal war in Southeast Asia. While Roger had left no explanatory statement, we can assume it was his intention to do with his own body what was a routine military event in Vietnam, the burning alive of human beings. I assured Merton that, had anyone at the Catholic Worker or CPF any idea that Roger was contemplating so desperate an action, no one would have let him out of sight for a single minute.

"I do not think," I added, "that Roger's suicide is going to have the dire effects you fear. The New York Chancery Office issued a simple statement to the effect that suicide is not permissible for Catholics and drew attention to Roger's confession before he died." The chaplain told reporters that Roger "made the most devout act of contrition I have ever heard—his voice was strong and he meant every word." Even the *New York Times* published a sympathetic editorial.

To give Merton a more three-dimensional view of what the daily life of CPF was all about as it approached its first birthday, I gave a tour of some of the mail currently on my desk: a membership application from a Benedictine monk with a letter describing the use the community was making of the CPF's conscientious objection folder with draft-age men staying at their guest house; a pair of letters, one from a Navy lieutenant, the other from a Marine reservist, asking for information about how to apply for CO discharges from the military; a packet from the editor of a French Catholic journal (himself a CPF member) containing recent declarations made during Vatican Council discussions of conscience and war-related topics; numerous appreciative letters to an article about Roger LaPorte that I had written for *Ave Maria*, a popular Catholic magazine; a contract from Macmillan for a *Catholic Worker* anthology that Tom and

I were editing;[4] a letter from a Catholic college in Los Angeles inviting a CPF speaker to give a lecture; several other lecture requests; a donation of $3,000 from a member in the Mid-West and a pledge of $2,000 from a supporter on the West Coast. I added that demand for our folder on conscientious objection had resulted in our having to order a new printing; only a few of the first printing of eight thousand copies were still on hand.

Finally I reminded Merton of the major CPF project of the moment, publication of a two-page statement headlined "Peace on Earth—Peace in Vietnam" that would appear in *Commonweal's* December 10 issue and soon after in several other national Catholic publications. Two hundred prominent Catholics, both lay and clergy, had signed.[5]

"This is," I wrote, "a fragmentary list, but does it not indicate that something of great moment is taking place—that the CPF is making a significant contribution in the American Catholic community?"

In his response, Merton reversed himself, deciding to remain a sponsor. He wrote at some length to explain what lay behind his initial withdrawal. One key factor was a major development in his own life that had occurred only ten weeks earlier. On August 20, after many years of letters, prayers, and petitions, Merton had finally been allowed to live full-time as a hermit. This meant considerably more solitude than had been possible before. He felt he

---

4. *A Penny a Copy: Readings from The Catholic Worker,* ed. Tom Cornell and Jim Forest (New York: Macmillan, 1968). A revised, updated edition, co-edited with Robert Ellsberg, was published by Orbis Books in 1995.

5. The CPF declaration began with a sentence from Pope John's encyclical *Pacem in terris*: "The right of every man to life is correlative with the duty to preserve it." The text attacked the character of the U.S.-sponsored governments in Vietnam, chastised the American government for failing to seriously pursue a peaceful settlement, and criticized the conduct of the war for failing to meet just war standards. Reports were cited of mass killings, torture, forced removal and relocation, defoliation, public executions without trial, and the indiscriminate killing of noncombatants. "The war in Vietnam has," it was stated, "unleashed weapons and tactics which are in violation of natural law and of the Gospel." The signers concluded that they could "neither defend nor support such a war."

was at last being freed to do the things he had longed for when he began his monastic life twenty-four years earlier. He envisioned a less cluttered life, fewer chores, less correspondence, and less public visibility.[6]

In reality the more hidden life he had imagined proved in some ways more exposed and more vulnerable. Merton felt the actions involving his Catholic pacifist friends in New York like an earthquake under his feet. He wrote:

I am really grateful for your long letter.... The whole package was a very great help indeed. I was happy to read Tom Cornell's lucid statement [in the November 19 Commonweal*], which is the first real information I have had on the positive arguments for card burning. I have been getting a very partial and rather alarmed set of reports on everything down here and my perspective has been way out. Your enclosures were very encouraging and I am happy about all that. Let me first of all apologize for the following things:*

1. For sending the telegram as a more or less emotional reflex, without really thinking the whole thing out.

2. For insinuating that the whole peace movement, including CPF, was operating in a climate of pathology. You are right, of course: the whole current reality has a lot of pathology in it, but the country is not nuts and the peace movement is not nuts either. You are making a lot of sense.

3. For blasting at you with what is really a personal problem of my own, at a time when you certainly had enough difficulties of your own to contend with. It was selfish of me and I am sorry.

I can see from your letter, the enclosures and [also] from letters of Dan Berrigan and Dorothy Day, that really God has used all this and His love has not been idle or refused in your hearts, in this very tragic

---

6. This was why he had not been listed as a signer of the CPF's Vietnam statement. "Now that the hermit project is getting underway," he had written me on the August 20, "I am especially restricted and have to watch everything I do that can be construed as looking back to the wicked world, such as thinking thoughts of peace" (HGL, 285).

and difficult trial. As for Roger, the picture I get of him is a very positive one. I am very sorry he had to do what he did but I am sure that as far as he is concerned nothing has been lost. . . .

Now to get back to my own difficulty. I suppose I was wrought up enough for it to take on the air of a formal public repudiation of CPF, but that is not really what I intended. I certainly don't want to make things difficult for you, and I would hardly want to interfere with the fine work you are doing for conscientious objectors.

My chief problem is, as I said before, personal. I am so to speak making my novitiate as a "hermit" of sorts and I have my hands full with this. It is a full-time job just coping with one's own damn mind in solitude, without getting wrought up about what appear to be the vagaries of others. Let's face the fact that my usefulness to CPF is at best purely symbolic, but it does nevertheless imply a heavy responsibility. There is no question that people, at least in this area, tend to hold me responsible for what you guys do. I know this because I am told it. It is of course more gossip, but they are associating the card burning with my ideas about peace. This certainly does not make life simple for me since I am not quite sure that I agree with card burning (though I accept Tom's arguments for his own position). At the same time it is not easy for me to find out just what the scoop is. This leaves me hanging on a hook not of my own choosing. . . .

If I thought of getting my name off your list of sponsors it was chiefly because of the embarrassment caused me by the inevitable fact that I am automatically blamed for whatever is done in your area of the peace movement, which means in practice for anything done by a Catholic Worker member too.

I am perfectly willing to leave the thing hanging in the balance for a while, so as not to create the impression that I am publicly denouncing you or throwing a wrench in your good work. But in any case I must sooner or later get in a position where it is clear that I am not accountable for what my friends do, and that I don't necessarily advocate all that is done by them.

Do you see my position? I think it would be clear and acceptable to all if it were understood that I was withdrawing from all such involve-

*ments, formally, without repudiating anyone personally. And without
repudiating the movement.*

*I am in no rush to do this, and I am willing to consider different
possibilities. But now I must end this letter, and I do so hoping you
understand that it is simply a personal matter of my own, not a "political" move of some sort. I would appreciate it if we could work this out
some way.*

*Again, I appreciated your letter very much indeed. It made a lot of
sense. And what you are doing is great. I admire the courage of Tom,
of Dave Miller and all those who are going through the struggle you
are going through.[7] I keep you in my prayers, and I hope it is possible
for me to say these things frankly without you getting the impression
that I am betraying you. I have enough confidence in your friendship
to hope that you will not interpret it in such a way.*

Merton changed his mind. This isn't a trait one takes for granted
in anyone. Not only did he change his mind, but he decided to make
a public statement about the new shape of his vocation and at the
same time to mention the reasons he would remain a CPF sponsor
even while pruning his life severely. The CPF released his statement
a few days before Christmas and it was widely reported in the press.
Beginning with a denial of the ever-current rumors that he had left
the monastery and abandoned the contemplative life, he said,

*In actual fact, far from abandoning the contemplative life, I have
received permission to go into it more deeply. I have been granted an
opportunity for greater solitude and more intense prayer, meditation
and study. As a result of this, I am even less involved in various activities than I was before. . . . I am not keeping track of current controversies. . . . I am not taking an active part in [the peace movement]. . . .*

*However, I certainly believe it is my duty to give at least general
and moral support to all forms of Catholic Action. . . . In particular, I*

---

7. A year later, while still not seeing draft-card burning as an appropriate tactic
for "big campaigns," in a joint letter to Tom and me Merton wrote, "The more I
think about the card burning, the more I think that you, Tom, are utterly right
before God" (HGL, 298; letter dated November 16, 1966).

continue to give . . . moral support to those who are working to imple-ment the teachings of the Council and of the modern Popes on war and peace. If my name remains among the sponsors of the Catholic Peace Fellowship, it is because I believe that this dedicated group is sin-cerely striving to spread the teachings of the Gospel and of the Church on war, peace, and the brotherhood of man. However, my sponsorship does not imply automatic approval of any and every move made by this group, still less of individual actions on the part of its members acting on their own responsibility. . . . I personally believe that what we need most of all today is patient, constructive and pastoral work rather than acts of defiance which antagonize the average person without enlightening him.[8]

Paradoxically, the final effect of Merton's short-lived resignation from the board of sponsors was that he became more visibly engaged with CPF while, in the background, he challenged us to more clearly define our "pastoral" work—that is, to help make far better known such papal statements as *Pacem in terris* and the council's *Constitution on the Church in the Modern World*. While the council and popes had spoken plainly and authoritatively, Merton pointed out, few if any American Catholic prelates were going to convey that message in a way that could be clearly understood by the average churchgoer, with the consequence that the Vietnam War would continue on its murderous course, with Catholics as engaged in the killing as any other group. Pope John's groundbreaking encyclical and the coun-cil's declarations on war and conscience would be dead letters unless the CPF got the message out to the colleges, the seminaries, the clergy, and young people facing the draft.

"This is a big job," Merton said. "It is what you are called to do now." While in some ways the task was colorless and undramatic— "simply reaching a lot of people and helping them to change their minds"—it could have a "transforming effect on the American

---

8. Written December 3, 1965; distributed by press release December 22. In the Thomas Merton Center archive in Louisville and the Catholic Peace Fellowship archive at the University of Notre Dame.

Icon of the Virgin and Child given to Merton
by Marco Pallis. (Photo by Jim Forest)

Catholic Church.... I think it is extremely important not to come out with some gesture that strikes the average Catholic as a needless provocation and drives him back into the arms of conservatism and inertia. In my opinion the job of the CPF is not so much to make a strong impression ... of being a very radical group ... but to reach the ordinary Catholic as far as possible, or at least the ones who are most open to the new look, without being very radical themselves. It is this that is going to make the big difference."[9]

Indeed the CPF's draft counseling plus its educational work on war and peace help explain the astonishing fact that the Catholic Church in the United States produced a major contingent of conscientious objectors during the Vietnam War. While I haven't succeeded in tracking down the final number, at the end of 1969, five years before the Vietnam War ended, out of 34,255 men who had registered as conscientious objectors, 2,494 identified themselves as Catholic.[10] By the time the war ended in 1975, given the fact that

9. HGL, 289-90; letter dated December 3, 1965.

10. See Patricia McNeal, "Catholic Conscientious Objection during World War II," *Catholic Historical Review* 61 (April 1975): 232.

opposition to it had steadily expanded, the number of conscientious objectors would at least have tripled.

In the midst of those intensely stressful days in the final weeks of 1965 it happened that a providential gift was delivered to Merton's hermitage: a hand-painted icon of the Virgin and Child. The donor was one of his friends-by-letter, Marco Pallis, a British-born son of Greek Orthodox parents who later in life encountered the Tibetan Buddhist tradition and became one of its most articulate interpreters, best known for his classic work, *Peaks and Lamas*. For Merton, the icon was like a kiss from God. He wrote Pallis in response:

> *How shall I begin? I have never received such a precious and magnificent gift from anyone in my life. I have no words to express how deeply moved I was to come face to face with this sacred and beautiful presence granted to me. . . . At first I could hardly believe it. . . . [This] icon of the Holy Mother came as a messenger at a precise moment when a message was needed, and her presence before me has been an incalculable aid in resolving a difficult problem.*
>
> *It is a perfect act of timeless worship. I never tire of gazing at it. There is a spiritual presence and reality about it, a true spiritual "Taboric" light,* [11] *which seems unaccountably to proceed from the Heart of the Virgin and Child as if they had One heart, and which goes out to the whole universe. It is unutterably splendid. And silent. It imposes a silence on the whole hermitage.* [12]

---

11. "Taboric," a term associated with the Hesychast tradition, refers to the "uncreated light" that radiated from Christ when he was transfigured on Mount Tabor. See Matthew 17:1-9; Mark 9:2-8; Luke 9:28-36; and 2 Peter 1:16-18.

12. HGL, 473-74; letter dated December 5, 1965.

A Quiet Voice at the Vatican Council

THE SECOND VATICAN COUNCIL, the convocation of all Catholic bishops that began in 1962 and ended shortly before Christmas three years later, was one of the major events of the twentieth century. Two thousand four hundred bishops took part plus observers from many churches, ranging from Quaker to Orthodox. In addition there were hundreds of *periti*—consultant theologians—who had been appointed by particular bishops. Pope John's great hope for the council was that it would "restore the simple and pure lines that the face of the Church of Jesus had at its birth." Remarkably, given that the participants had a great deal to disagree about, the council proved to be a giant step toward achievement of that elusive goal.

Even though he was seven time zones away from Rome, Merton took an active part in the council through correspondence and the circulation of his writings.

While welcoming Pope John's surprising decision to convene such a gathering, Merton did not take for granted that the council would meet the great expectations it had quickly generated. "The Council has got to fulfill great hopes or be a disaster," he wrote in a letter to publisher Frank Sheed in 1962. "It is absolutely no use reaffirming the disciplinary and juridical positions that have been affirmed one way or another for a thousand years."[1]

One of Merton's worries was that many of the bishops, their views influenced by national priorities and outlooks, would oppose a blanket condemnation of methods of war, nuclear and otherwise, in which the casualties were chiefly noncombatants, nor would they support a text that gave the individual citizen the right—under some circumstances the duty—to refuse military service.

---

1. *Witness to Freedom* (WTF), 45; letter dated March 1962.

Catholic bishops gather for the Second Vatican Council.

If many American bishops were strong supporters of U.S. military policies, there were others who had a perspective similar to Merton's. One of these was John Wright, bishop of Pittsburgh, who shared copies of *Peace in the Post-Christian Era* and other Merton writings with his fellow bishops as well as with theologians assisting them.[2] During the final session of the council in 1965, Wright wrote to Merton with the news that the matters that especially concerned both of them were going well. He then added: "I sat in a Roman barber shop next to a man who was reading an Italian translation of one of your books. . . . I said to him that I know you, and he said '*Dica lui per me, grazie.*' [Say thanks to him for me.] So *grazie.*"[3]

Merton wrote to Wright in July 1965:

2. In 1970 Wright was made a cardinal by Pope Paul VI and appointed to head the Roman Congregation of the Clergy.

3. HGL, 608.

> *As you know, I feel very strongly (and I believe you do too) that the question of war, of modern war technology, and of the right to refuse participation in massive and unjust use of force, all amounts to a kind of exposed nerve in the operation of Christian renewal. I frankly think the ability of the Council [to address these issues] with tact and understanding . . . will determine the reality of the renewal that has been so convincingly proposed so far.*

On the other hand, Merton warned:

> *[Even implicit acceptance of modern war technology] would have the most serious pastoral consequences, in effect binding Catholics to participate in any and every war, to assent to and cooperate with any and every means which a government may decide . . . to be expedient. . . . It would be a disaster if the Council simply made a statement that left Christians at the mercy of . . . power structures, under the pretext that this is sufficient obedience to God.*[4]

Among Merton's links to Rome were Hildegard Goss-Mayr and her husband, Jean Goss, co-secretaries of the International Fellowship of Reconciliation. Though based in Vienna, the two were often in Rome where they labored to put war, conscientious objection, and nonviolence on the council agenda. In a journal entry dated December 17, 1962, Merton noted that earlier in the day he had sent three packets of his peace writings to the Goss-Mayrs, who remarkably had been given permission by Dom Gabriel Sortais, the Trappist abbot general, to "present [Merton's writings] for consideration by the Council Fathers and theologians who are perhaps to prepare a schema [draft text] on nuclear war for the Council."[5]

One of the Goss-Mayrs' most sympathetic and helpful contacts at the Vatican was none other than Cardinal Alfredo Ottaviani, head of the Holy Office and one of the key figures responsible for laying the groundwork for the council. Ottaviani was so often

---

4. HGL, 610-11; letter dated July 17, 1965.
5. TTW, 276.

described by journalists as "the *archconservative* Cardinal Ottaviani" that the adjective nearly became part of his title. It was widely assumed that he was the defender of all that was in urgent need of reformation in the Catholic Church. What many did not know was that the cardinal was so conservative that, rigorously applying the just war doctrine to the grim realities of modern warfare, he regarded all war as immoral and had great respect for those refusing military service. (At the end of his first meeting with Jean Goss in 1962, Ottaviani gave Jean a solemn blessing not only for himself as an individual conscientious objector but on behalf of *all* conscientious objectors.)

Another Merton collaborator at the council was Archbishop Thomas Roberts, an English Jesuit who formerly headed the archdiocese of Bombay in India, a post he had left so that it might be taken up by an Indian. Roberts's sense of humor was legendary. He once described the council as "a football match at which all the players are bishops." During the council, he made a widely reported intervention on conscientious objection that drew attention to the witness given by Franz Jägerstätter:

> *What we must do here is to give clear testimony that the Church affirms the right of the individual conscience to refuse unjust military service and assure those of the Faithful, who bear such witness, that they will always have her full support. Once this has been done, martyrs like Franz Jägerstätter will never again have to feel that they take their stand alone.... Perhaps the major scandal of Christianity for too many centuries now has been precisely that almost every war has allowed itself to become the moral arms of its own government, even in war later recognized as palpably unjust. Let us break with this tragic past by making a clear and unambiguous affirmation of the right and obligation of each Christian to obey the voice of his or her informed conscience before and during a time of war.*[6]

---

6. https://walktheway.wordpress.com/2011/02/28/an-extraordinary-jesuit-archbishop.

Still another Merton contact, James Douglass, was in Rome throughout much of the council, initially to pursue doctoral studies at the Gregorian University but in the end working as a theological advisor on questions of war and peace to several American, British and Swedish bishops, plus Abbot Christopher Butler of Downside Abbey in England,[7] a member of the commission drafting the chapter of Schema 13 that included the section on war.[8]

At the end of the council's third session, Bishop John Taylor of Stockholm, one of the bishops Douglass was assisting, submitted an intervention on Schema 13 that began with a reference to Merton:

> *Thomas Merton, one of the most profound mystical theologians of our times, has written that total nuclear war would be a sin of mankind equal only to the crucifixion of Christ. Modern means of war threaten the very existence of man. Moreover, the Council has a sacred duty to respond with all its moral power to this threat of mankind's self-destruction.*

The fourth and final session of the council began in September 1965 and continued for three months. Its major work was completing Schema 13, as it was known in the drafting stage, or *Gaudium et spes* [GS], the Latin words for "joy and hope" with which the *Pastoral Constitution on the Church in the Modern World* begins.

Shortly before the last session began, Merton wrote an "open letter" to the American hierarchy in which he urged the bishops to rise above national interests:

> *The Christian is called, as always, to a decision for Christ, not to a decision for this or that kind of society. He is called to obey the Gospel of love, for all men, and not simply to devote himself to the interests of a nation, a party, a class, or a culture.*
>
> *We must be resolutely convinced that this is one area in which the Church is bound not only to disagree with "the world" in the most*

---

7. Later Butler was appointed auxiliary bishop of Westminster, the Catholic archdiocese in the British capital.

8. Douglass wrote at length about peace work at the council in *The Non-Violent Cross* (New York: Macmillan, 1968), 100-136.

forceful terms, but intervene as a providentially designated force for peace and reconciliation. We must clearly recognize that the Church remains perhaps the most effective single voice speaking for peace in the world today. That voice must not be silenced or made ineffective by any ambiguity born of political and pragmatic considerations on the part of national groups.

In time of war, Merton noted, "the average citizen [feels he] has no choice but to support his government and bear arms if called upon to do so," as was seen in World War II with the compliant participation of German Catholics "in a war effort that has since revealed itself to have been a monstrously criminal and unjust aggression." And, he added, as the war unfolded and the tactics of the Allies moved from precision bombing of military targets to city destruction,

[T]hose who defended their nations in a manifestly just resistance . . . eventually found themselves unknowingly cooperating in acts of total, indiscriminate and calculatedly terroristic destruction which Christian morality cannot tolerate.

Merton appealed to the bishops to make an unambiguous statement advocating the renunciation of violence in favor of negotiations and other nonviolent means of conflict settlement. Methods of warfare that result in the indiscriminate killing of both combatants and noncombatants must be unreservedly condemned.

The common man, the poor man, the man who has no hope but in God, everywhere looks to the Church as a last hope of protection against the unprincipled machinations of militarists and power politicians.

Merton concluded his letter with a challenge:

What matters is for the bishops and the Council to bear witness clearly and without any confusion to the Church's belief in the power of love to save and transform not only individuals but society. Do we believe or do we not that love has this power? If we believe it, what point is there in splitting hairs about the superior morality of killing a thousand defenseless non-combatants rather than a million?[9]

---

9. WTF, 88-92.

In addition to its circulation at the Council, Merton's "open letter" was published in the journal *Worldview* and distributed via his extensive network of friends. Merton also included the statement with a letter sent to Pope Paul VI.[10]

What Merton had hoped and prayed for was, to an astonishing extent, realized. The finished text of *Gaudium et spes* was given overwhelming support by the council fathers, with more than two thousand bishops approving the text, only seventy-five opposing. On December 7, 1965 the Constitution was signed and released to the world by Pope Paul VI. Though work on the text had been far from easy, unquestionably it was one of the council's crowning achievements. In fact, commented Father Francis X. Murphy (writing under the pen name Xavier Rynne), "no other conciliar document had gone through so many stages before reaching its final form."[11]

Gaudium et spes contained the one solemn condemnation issued by the Second Vatican Council:

> *Every act of war directed to the indiscriminate destruction of whole cities or vast areas with their inhabitants is a crime against God and humanity, which merits firm and unequivocal condemnation.*[12]

Of similar significance was the council's treatment of conscience:

> *In the depths of his conscience, man detects a law which he does not impose upon himself, but which holds him to obedience. Always sum-*

---

10. HGL, 490.

11. Xavier Rynne, *The Third Session* (New York: Farrar, Straus and Giroux, 1966), 116-17.

12. Section 80. The later archbishop of New Orleans, Philip Hannan, then auxiliary bishop of Washington, DC, led an unsuccessful effort to reject the section of Schema 13 that condemned weapons of mass destruction. He argued that the deterrent effect of nuclear armaments under the command of Western powers had "preserved freedom for a very large portion of the world." Even the use of nuclear weapons, he argued at the council, should not be condemned: "There now exist nuclear weapons which have a very precise limit of destruction. . . . It may be permitted to use these arms, with their limited effect, against military objectives in a just war according to theological principles."

moning him to love good and avoid evil, the voice of conscience when necessary speaks to his heart more specifically: do this, shun that. For man has in his heart a law written by God; to obey it is the very dignity of man; according to it he will be judged. Conscience is the most secret core and sanctuary of man. There he is alone with God whose voice echoes in his depths. In a wonderful manner conscience reveals that law which is fulfilled by love of God and neighbor. In fidelity to conscience, Christians are joined with the rest of men in the search for truth, and for the genuine solution of the numerous problems which arise in the lives of individuals and from social relationships. Hence, the more right conscience holds sway, the more persons and groups turn aside from blind choice and strive to be guided by objective norms of morality. Conscience frequently errs from individual ignorance without losing its dignity. The same cannot be said for a man who cares little for truth and goodness, or for conscience which by degrees grows practically sightless as a result of habitual sin. (GS, §16)

It follows that conscientious objection to participation in war ought to be universally recognized and respected:

It seems right that laws make humane provision for the case of those who for reasons of conscience refuse to bear arms, provided, however, that they agree to serve the human community in some other way. (GS, §79)

The express recognition of conscientious objection marked a major turning point in church teaching. For centuries, Catholics in every country had been told to obey their rulers and submit to conscription, assuring them that, were they made party to a sin by their obedience, the guilt would lie with the rulers rather than with their obedient subjects.

Those who obey commands that condemn the innocent and defenseless to death were described as "criminal":

Contemplating this melancholy state of humanity, the council wishes, above all things else, to recall the permanent binding force of universal natural law and its all-embracing principles. Man's conscience itself gives ever more emphatic voice to these principles. Therefore, actions which deliberately conflict with these same principles, as well as orders commanding such actions are criminal, and blind obedience cannot excuse those who yield to them. The most infamous among these are actions designed for the methodical extermination of an entire people, nation or ethnic minority. Such actions must be vehemently condemned as horrendous crimes. The courage of those who fearlessly and openly resist those who issue such commands merits supreme commendation. (GS, §79)

Those who renounce violence altogether, seeking to build a more just and compassionate society by nonviolent means, were applauded:

We cannot fail to praise those who renounce the use of violence in vindication of their rights and who resort to methods of defense which are otherwise available to weaker parties too, provided this can be done without injury to the rights and duties of others or to the community itself. (GS, §78)

With the publication first of *Pacem in terris* and then *Gaudium et spes*, the Catholic Church crossed a border. It had condemned nuclear war and indeed any sort of war in which noncombatants were targeted. At the same time it could no longer be presumed that obedience to national leaders would be the automatic response of faithful Catholics. It was no wonder that during the Vietnam War so many young American Catholics refused to take part.

Shortly after the council ended Bishop John Taylor of Stockholm presented Tom Cornell with the especially cast commemorative medallion given to each bishop who participated in the council. Taylor described his transfer of the gift as a gesture of thanks for "the role that the Catholic Peace Fellowship, together with the Catholic Worker, played at the Council—the role of invisible Council Father."

The medal might equally have been given to another invisible council father, Thomas Merton. What he had attempted to say in his banned book in 1962 had become the official teaching of the Catholic Church in 1965.

The end of the council and passage of *Gaudium et spes* refueled Merton's imagination regarding the future work of the CPF. In a long letter sent three days before New Year, he stressed that it was unlikely that the American hierarchy would develop programs to make known what the council had said about war and peace. "Obviously, the Hannans and Spellmans are not going to do much with the parts that have any bite and call for any substantial change of thought," he wrote. Small organization though it was, a major part of the job therefore fell to CPF, whose priority should be reaching out to Catholic colleges, seminaries, and the clergy. Merton volunteered to prepare the text for a leaflet "simply spelling out the Council teaching on war." He would, he said, soon be sending us a commentary on the key council texts that "goes over the whole Constitution and stresses the basic principles, personalism and the unity of the human family, on which the whole thing is built up."[13]

Merton continued:

> *I am personally convinced that this is the big chance for CPF to really do something important for the Church ... [even] much more important than [the] CW can do. ... I share your immense respect for [the Catholic Worker] and its prophetic quality, but precisely because it is prophetic it remains more or less a symbol that everyone admires and stays away from. Your more colorless and less dramatic job is apostolic: simply reaching a lot of people and helping them to change their minds. ... The thing about this particular task is that it is not in the least ambiguous. It is the straight teaching of the Church which [every committed Catholic] is bound to listen to. ... Your job is ... simply to get the Constitution [on the Church in the Modern World] across, not even worrying about whether or not it gets CPF better known and*

---

13. HGL, 290-93; letter to Jim Forest dated December 29, 1965. The commentary, entitled "The Church and the Godless World," was published in *Redeeming the Time* (London: Burns & Oates, 1966), 7-92, the British version of *Seeds of Destruction*.

so on. Just get people thinking in terms of that Constitution. That alone will be enough to justify anyone's existence in this life. Any help I can give, I will gladly give, within my limitations.

Once again Merton urged us to avoid "provocative actions" by which he meant "actions that have an aggressive, challenging nature over and above the simple question of conscience that is involved." However, he added, protest actions were not necessarily provocative in his sense of the term. For example

(Photo by Jim Forest)

"the Peace March in Washington in November, from what I heard about it, was not in any sense provocative, though it was a determined statement against the war in Vietnam."

Merton added that he had changed his mind about draft-card burnings now that he better understood the issues involved. He now realized that the law criminalizing draft-card burning was chiefly "aimed at silencing protest" and was "an example of provocative use of authority." Even so, he continued:

I still do not think that the dramatic and provocative type of witness is what we most need now, in the sphere of Catholic peace witness. On the contrary, I think what we need is massive and undramatic apostolic work to clarify the Church's teaching and get it thoroughly known. In this I think we should avoid as far as possible any dramatization of conflict between conservatives and liberals. . . . The more we can work along on the assumption that the whole Church is united . . . the better chance we have of getting this Constitution understood, and making the first step toward an abolition of war or a renunciation of the war mentality by everyone. The job is titanic.

For all the opposition the council's condemnation of modern war faced, Merton was convinced that many were prepared to listen:

As you know better than I, the country is full of sincere people who are honestly bothered by the killing in Vietnam and cannot see it as a just war, yet cannot identify themselves with a specifically pacifist protest. These people are morally in no-man's-land, under pressure from both extremes. These are the ones who need help in articulating their objections in terms of the Church's teachings. I think they must be reached in such a way that their refusal to be identified as pacifists is fully respected, above all because the Constitution's position is simply Catholic, and nothing else. No further label is required. People should understand this first of all.

The next thing is I think to begin a study of the pervasive violence that is everywhere in our thinking. This is the thing that I think is most dangerous, and humanly speaking I think it makes one almost despair of this nation being a peaceful one: we are a nation addicted to images of violence, brutality, sadism, self-affirmation by arrogance, aggression, and so on. . . .

On the other hand, behind all this aggressiveness is fear.[14] *Once these people are sure they are not being attacked, undermined and ruined, they are willing to listen to reason. The job is to get a hearing, a real hearing.*[15]

---

14. Here Merton echoes the theme of his first antiwar essay as published by *The Catholic Worker* four years earlier, "The Root of War Is Fear."

15. HGL, 293.

Saying No to War,
Loving Our Enemies

IN SEVERAL LETTERS MERTON described the work the Catholic
Peace Fellowship was called to carry out as "apostolic," from the
Greek word "*apostolos*"—a messenger. In a Christian context, it suggests carrying on the work of Christ's apostles, his trusted message-
bearers, the deliverers of news about how to live in the kingdom of
God. The kingdom of God, it turns out, is not a domain that Caesar
is pleased to see his subjects join for the simple reason that participation in it places obedience to God over obedience to Caesar. The
faithful Christian becomes free enough to say no and even suffer and
die for his no-saying. He or she can refuse to be enslaved by war.
Such indeed was the witness of the early church. Today, just as it was
twenty centuries ago, it's hard to disobey or even imagine doing so.
Caesar was and remains both persuasive and punitive.

The core message of the CPF during the Vietnam War was that
one can refuse to play a part in killing Vietnamese people. Once the
Vatican Council concluded its work in December 1965, one of CPF's
main projects was to significantly expand its two-page CO folder. In
April 1966 we published "Catholics and Conscientious Objection,"
a sixteen-page booklet which I wrote with guidance from members
of the CPF board of sponsors. The finished product was a slim document designed to fit in a standard business envelope and cost fifteen
cents.

The drafting process involved many readers—Merton was one of
them:

> *The pamphlet for [conscientious] objectors is very good, I think, [and]*
> *makes good use of the Council Constitution. The sensitive spot is [the*
> *section] on non-cooperation [with the draft]. I think you should go*

over that paragraph carefully. As it stands, there is nothing to enlighten the average priest ... about the legitimacy of such a position from the Catholic viewpoint. I think specifically Catholic arguments should be stated somehow. It should be stated clearly that non-cooperation with a law that one considers unjust is legitimate; and reasons why the selective service law might seem to some an unjust law. . . . Perhaps the one sentence that counts is the one where it says that the law does not really provide effectively for different forms of objection. I think there it should be stated clearly that: 'The selective service law as it now stands was framed with members of the traditional "Peace Churches" in view, that is to say for those who believe, as part of their religion, that all war is always immoral. Hence it fails to provide for those who discriminate between just and unjust wars, as many Catholic objectors do.' Something like that.[1]

Several revisions were required—every word mattered; every quotation and fact had to be carefully checked. The finished text presented the nonviolent teaching and witness of the church in its first four centuries as well as the gradual emergence of the "just war" doctrine from the time of Saint Augustine onward, including the strict conditions that must be met for a war to be regarded as just. There were declarations on war and peace from recent popes and fresh-out-of-the-oven quotations from the council's *Constitution on the Church in the Modern World*. We told the stories of such great saints as Martin of Tours, who had confronted Caesar—in Martin's case face-to-face before Julius Caesar—with the words, "I am a soldier of Christ; to fight is not permissible for me." (Remarkably Saint Martin, though briefly imprisoned, was not martyred and went on to become a missionary bishop. Many churches in Europe bear his name.) Information about the varieties of conscientious objection and draft-board procedures was included.[2]

---

1. HGL, 294; letter dated January 17, 1966.

2. The booklet's text is posted here: http://jimandnancyforest.com/2015/08/catholics-and-conscientious-objection. It also exists in a modified form intended for Orthodox Christians: http://incommunion.org/2005/08/06/orthodox-christians-and-conscientious-objection.

As we neared completion of the manuscript in January 1966, Tom Cornell proposed we seek formal ecclesiastical approbation, as it would go far in widening the booklet's impact and circulation. Though not optimistic about the result, we applied for an *imprimatur* from the Archdiocese of New York, at the time headed by Cardinal Francis Spellman, one of the bishops most supportive of the Vietnam War and least sympathetic to conscientious objection. To our astonishment, in March 1966 the *imprimatur* was given. In fact the diocesan censor, Monsignor John Goodwine, professor of moral theology and canon law at Saint Joseph's Seminary in Dunwoodie, NY, played a helpful role, making suggestions that improved several passages. Thanks to the *imprimatur*, the booklet made its ways into Catholic parishes, schools, seminaries, and universities where previously anything along such lines would have landed in the wastebasket.

On the inside cover, just above the *imprimatur*, was a statement from Dom Christopher Butler, abbot of Downside, a renowned Benedictine Abbey in England:

> *Let us take this opportunity of saying clearly that the Church ... does not seek protection from its enemies, whoever these may be, in war, and especially not war of the modern type. We are the Mystical Body and Christ is our Head. He refused to defend himself and his mission by the swords of his disciples or even by legions of angels, the ministers of God's justice and love. The weapons of the Gospel are not nuclear but spiritual, and it wins its victories not by war but by suffering. . . . Good ends do not justify immoral means, nor do they justify even a conditional intention of meeting immoral attack with immoral defense. Our help is in the name of the Lord, who made heaven and earth.*

The text on page one began with an understatement:

> *The Catholic attempting to discover the Church's teaching on war may find himself confronted with historical and theological confusion. On the one hand we are clearly enjoined to love our enemies as ourselves; we are under orders to feed our enemy if he hungers, to provide drink if he thirsts. On the other hand, the vast majority of Catholics have, for*

seventeen centuries, taken an active part in their nation's wars, often battling each other.

A boxed quotation from President Kennedy appeared elsewhere in the booklet:

War will exist until that distant day when the conscientious objector enjoys the same reputation and prestige the warrior does today.[3]

In its last section, the booklet argued against blind obedience:

It is now clear that none of us can any longer accept as God's will what congressmen, generals and draft officials might wish of us. Unthinking obedience has at last been made to stand without a virtuous or even patriotic façade. Our concepts, both regarding love of man and love of native land, have been considerably enriched and expanded. In the words of the Second Vatican Council, we have learned that "human dignity demands that each person act according to a free choice that is personally motivated and prompted from within, not under blind internal impulse nor by mere external pressures."[4] We have come to realize, though sometimes at great cost in suffering, that freedom and happiness ultimately spring from the individual's willingness to take responsibility for the use of his life.

Fifty-thousand copies of the booklet were distributed in the first year. During the decade-long Vietnam War, more than 300,000 copies of the booklet were sold or given away.

In 1965, about the time I was writing "Catholics and Conscientious Objection," Merton was writing "St. Maximus the Confessor on Nonviolence."[5] One of the essay's emphases was the love of enemies:

Christians are sometimes so disturbed by the enemies of Christianity that they become convinced that hatred of these enemies is proof of

---

3. Letter to a Navy friend, quoted in Arthur M. Schlesinger, Jr., *A Thousand Days: John F. Kennedy in the White House* (Boston: Houghton Mifflin, 1965), 88.

4. *Constitution on the Church in the Modern World,* §17.

5. St. Maximus the Confessor (ca. 580-662) is recognized as a father of the church.

their love for Christ, and that the will to destroy them is a pledge of their own salvation. At such a time it is necessary to go back to the sources and try to recover the true Christian meaning of the first and all-embracing commandment to love all men including our enemies. Failure to understand and observe this commandment brings down the wrath of God on our civilization. . . . [The love of enemies] is not merely a theoretical matter. . . . It is on the contrary one of the crucial ways in which we give proof in practice that we are truly disciples of Christ.[6]

A major obstacle to loving one's enemies, Merton continued, is the sad fact that many Christians are more attached to property than to people. "It is because we love money, possessions, comforts . . . that we enter into conflict with our fellow man." Thus the importance of voluntary poverty in order to more readily open the door to both stranger and adversary.

There are those, Merton noted, who dismiss the love of enemies as patently absurd and impossible. Surely such teaching is for the exceptional—for monks and nuns and the would-be saint—not ordinary people. For such reasons many Christians abandon the most basic of Christ's commandments.[7]

Maximus the Confessor, Merton wrote, addressed the problem by imagining a dialogue between a master and a disciple. The disciple questions the possibility of loving one's enemies. The master responds by pointing out that if it were impossible to love one's enemies, God would not have commanded it. We have only to consider the lives of the many Christians who have taken the commandment seriously, Merton explained, echoing Maximus. Even more persuasive is the example of Jesus:

Instead of hating His enemies, the Lord continued to love them and even laid down His life for them.

---

6. "St. Maximus the Confessor on Non-Violence" was published in the September 1965 issue of *The Catholic Worker*. The text is included in PFP, 241-47.

7. My own treatment of the topic is in *Loving Our Enemies: Reflections on the Hardest Commandment* (Maryknoll, NY: Orbis Books, 2015).

The point, Merton wrote, is this:

A superficial and even illusionary Christianity is one which professes faith in Christ by verbal formulas and external observance, but which in fact denies Christ by refusing to obey His commandment to love. Since no man can serve two masters, and since the Christian life is a bitter struggle to keep the commandments of Christ in spite of everything in order to hold fast to our faith in Him and not deny Him, the enemy of Christ seeks in every way to make us deny the Lord in our lives and in our actions, even though we may remain apparently faithful to Him in our words and in our worship. He does this by leading us to hate others on account of our attachment to money and pleasure or, when [like a monk] we have apparently renounced these, to hate others when they attack us in our own person or in the society to which we belong. But in all these cases we must see that the evil that is done to us, apparently, by others, is a summons to greater faith and to heroic obedience to the word of the Gospel.[8]

---

8. PFP, 247.

Face to Face with Vietnam

BESIDES HIS PEACE WRITINGS and the advisory role he played with
the Catholic Peace Fellowship, Merton was intensely involved in
a form of more intimate peace work: building bridges of dialogue
between Catholic and non-Catholic Christians, both Orthodox and
Protestant, and also developing friendships with Buddhists, Jews,
Hindus, Taoists, and Sufis.[1] It was an aspect of Merton that Pope
Francis highlighted in his address to the U.S. Congress in 2015:
"[Thomas Merton] was also a man of dialogue, a promoter of peace
between peoples and religions."

While this dimension of his life took off in the sixties, its roots
went back at least to 1938, the year a Hindu monk named Bramachari entered Merton's life while he was a graduate student at Columbia. Bramachari had been sent from his ashram in India to take part
in a Congress of Religions at the World's Fair in Chicago, but had
arrived too late. Staying on in America anyway, he was in New York
thanks to Merton's friends, Sy and Helen Freedgood, living quietly
in their home despite the presence of a grandmother who worried
that this Asian in turban, white robes, and tattered sneakers might be
an enemy of the Jewish people.

Merton spent long hours talking with Bramachari. "He was never
sarcastic, never ironical or unkind in his criticisms: in fact he did
not make many judgments at all, especially adverse ones," Merton recalled. "He would simply make statements of fact, and then
burst out laughing—his laughter was quiet and ingenuous, and it

---

1. Fons Vitae has published a series of books that explore these areas of engagement in depth: *Merton and Buddhism, Merton and Judaism, Merton and Hesychasm*
(on the spirituality of Eastern Christianity), *Merton and Sufism,* and *Merton and
the Tao.*

expressed his complete amazement at the very possibility that people should live the way he saw them living all around him."[2]

Americans often asked Bramachari about the progress of Christian missionaries in India. Bramachari's response impressed Merton. The big problem was, he said, that they lived too comfortably, "in a way that simply made it impossible for Hindus to regard them as holy—let alone the fact that they ate meat." Hindus were amazed that Christians weren't ascetics.

For all his criticisms of missionaries, Bramachari played a missionary role in Merton's life. "He did not generally put his words in the form of advice," Merton recalled, "but the one counsel he did give me is something that I will not easily forget: 'There are many beautiful mystical books written by the Christians. You should read Saint Augustine's *Confessions*, and *The Imitation of Christ*.... Yes, you must read those books.'" Merton did as Bramachari advised. As *The Seven Storey Mountain* bears witness, the books a Hindu monk had urged him to study played a part in Merton's reception into the Catholic Church before the year had ended.

In May 1966 Merton welcomed a visitor to his hermitage, Thich Nhat Hanh, a brown-robed Zen Buddhist monk from Vietnam.[3] Perhaps his Vietnamese guest reminded him of Bramachari. Both respected Christianity, and both had a playful aspect. One of the principal figures in Vietnam's peace movement, Nhat Hanh was also the leading figure in the development of "engaged Buddhism," a pathway that linked insights gained from meditation and the teachings of the Buddha to situations of suffering and injustice. Nhat Hanh was founder of a movement of service in Vietnamese villages, The School of Youth for Social Service. One of the precepts of a rule Nhat Hanh had written called on his disciples: "Do not avoid suffering or close your eyes before suffering. Do not lose awareness of the existence of suffering in the life of the world. Find ways to

---

2. SSM, 196.

3. Accompanying Nhat Hanh for that visit was John Heidbrink, staff member of the Fellowship of Reconciliation, the group responsible for arranging Nhat Hanh's U.S. travels.

be with those who are suffering, including personal contact, visits, images and sounds. By such means, awaken yourself and others to the reality of suffering in the world."[4]

At immense personal risk, many Vietnamese Buddhists had peacefully resisted the war and had worked toward a "third way" solution that sought a negotiated end to the civil war and the exodus of American soldiers. Because of the horrors of the war, Nhat Hanh had temporarily given up many of the externals of the monastic life in order to act as a spokesman for the war's victims, though the reality of his contemplative identity remained unimpaired.

Vietnamese monk Thich Nhat Hanh. (Photo by Jim Forest)

Thich Nhat Hanh is "a perfectly formed monk," Merton said to his novices the day after the two-day visit ended, telling them that his Vietnamese guest's arrival was really the answer to a prayer.

In meeting Nhat Hanh, Merton had met Vietnam.

At the time of their encounter Merton's interest in Eastern spirituality was already well developed. *The Way of Chuang Tzu* had been published a year earlier while much of the content of *Mystics and Zen Masters,* to appear in 1967, had already been written. Another book, *Zen and the Birds of Appetite,* would go to press in 1968. Merton had both corresponded with and met with D. T. Suzuki, a Japanese exponent of Zen. But he had known nothing of the development of socially engaged Buddhism in Vietnam until Nhat Hanh's arrival. The two monks stayed up into the night, sharing the chant of their respective traditions, discussing methods of prayer and meditation, comparing Western and Eastern aspects of monastic life, and talking about the war.

---

4. http://viewonbuddhism.org/resources/14_precepts.html.

"What is the war like?" Merton had asked. "Everything is destroyed," Nhat Hanh replied. These three words, Merton told his novices, were the compact answer of a true monk—not a long-winded analysis but just the essence: "Everything is destroyed."

It was also a poet's answer. Like Merton, Nhat Hanh was a poet.

One aspect of their conversation concerned the formation of young monks, a process that in Vietnam begins not in a novitiate classroom but in the monastery kitchen and gardens, where the novice may feel he is nothing more than an unpaid laborer ignored by everyone. Unbeknownst to the novice, in fact he is being quietly watched by an elder who, once he has come to know the novice without exchanging a word, at last reveals himself as a spiritual parent. Only then does spoken conversation and guidance begin.

Monastic formation, both Buddhist and Christian, has much to do with discovering the significance of "insignificant" moments and the most routine activities: washing dishes, cutting vegetables, pulling weeds, sweeping floors, waiting in line, walking from here to there. It is an attitude Nhat Hanh sums up in one word: mindfulness. For example, it doesn't help to rush from a "less sacred" to a "more sacred" part of the monastery where, once you arrive, you change gears and move more reverently. "Before you can meditate," Nhat Hanh told Merton and Merton told the novices, "you must learn how to close the door." Aware of how often they ran to the church in order to be on time to chant the monastic offices, leaving behind them a trail of slammed doors, the novices laughed.[5]

Nhat Hanh, Merton commented, is an example of a true monk who cannot ignore a social crisis in the world around him but is "professionally involved" simply because a monk sees and hears. "A genuine monk has an orientation toward peace and a reverence for life," Merton said. "He tries to save whatever he can."

---

5. Thomas Merton Center, monastic conference recordings, CD-164-3, recorded May 29, 1966. My account draws on both the recording of Merton's talk to the novices and my own conversations with Nhat Hanh when I was living with him in Paris.

Thich Nhat Hanh with Thomas Merton.
(Photo by John Heidbrink)

After the visit ended Merton wrote a declaration about his newly found "brother":

Thich Nhat Hanh is my brother. This is not a political statement. It has no "interested" motive, it seeks to provoke no immediate reaction "for" or "against" this or that side in the Vietnam war. It is on the contrary a human and personal statement and an anguished plea for the Vietnamese Buddhist monk Thich Nhat Hanh who is my brother. He is more my brother than many who are nearer to me in race and nationality, because he and I see things exactly the same way. He and I deplore the war for exactly the same reasons . . . reasons of sanity, justice and love. We deplore the needless destruction, the . . . ravaging of human life, the rape of the culture. . . . [6]

Merton underscored the fact that neither he nor Nhat Hanh were political in the ordinary sense. They supported no political ideology. In fact no armed side tolerates a spokesman for toleration—"with one message, he betrays both sides. He does so simply because he speaks for compassion."

Merton stressed that Nhat Hanh had risked his life in order to present the war's reality to Americans, presenting "a picture which is not given to us in our newspapers and magazines." He is doing the work of a witness:

> *Nhat Hanh is a free man . . . moved by the spiritual dynamic of a tradition of religious compassion. He has come among us as many others have, from time to time, bearing witness to the spirit of Zen. More than any other he has shown us that Zen is not an esoteric and world-denying cult of inner illumination, but that it has its rare and unique sense of responsibility for the modern world. Wherever he goes he will walk in the strength of his spirit and in the solitude of the Zen monk who sees beyond life and death. . . .*
>
> *I have said that Nhat Hanh is my brother, and it is true. We are both monks, and we have lived the monastic life about the same number of years. We are both poets, both existentialists. I have far more in common with Nhat Hanh than I have with many Americans, and do not hesitate to say it. It is vitally important that such bonds be admitted. They are the bonds of a new solidarity and a new brotherhood which is beginning to be evident on all the five continents and which cuts across all political, religious and cultural lines to unite young men and women in every country in something that is more concrete than an ideal and more alive than a program. The unity of the young is the only hope for the world. In its name I appeal for Nhat Hanh. Do what you can for him. If I mean something to you, then let me put it this*

---

6. "Thich Nhat Hanh Is My Brother" was first published in *Jubilee*, August 1966 (PFP, 260-62).

way: do for Nhat Hanh whatever you would do for me if I were in his position. In many ways I wish I were.

Their conversations strengthened Merton in the conviction that the peacemaker is one who rejects victories by sides but, instead, seeks reconciliation and is committed to the formation of a community that protects the economic, cultural, political, and spiritual rights of each person and group within the disciplines of nonviolence.

This was the goal of Vietnam's third-way Buddhists. It meant an alternative to the absolutist claims and the military "solutions" of the competing sides. The third-way approach had immense implications, Nhat Hanh stressed, not only for the Vietnamese people but for the entire world and its fragile future.

Late in June Merton wrote a letter supporting the nomination of Thich Nhat Hanh for the Nobel Peace Prize:

> [*Thich Nhat Hanh*] *struck everyone he met here as a true messenger of peace and of spiritual values.* [*His visit*] *to the United States, to plead for peace in the awful war that is uselessly ravaging his country, has been one of the few really constructive and hopeful measures taken in this direction since the speech of Pope Paul VI at the United Nations. . . . Thich Nhat Hanh made this journey and delivered his message of peace at the risk of his own life. . . . There is considerable fear that he may be imprisoned and even killed* [*when he returns to Vietnam*] *as a result of his efforts for peace. It seems to me that he is eminently worthy, on the highest moral grounds, of consideration for the Peace Prize on account of the heroic character of his witness for peace.*

For Merton the encounter with Nhat Hanh was an encounter with a monk who carried his hermitage invisibly around him, a contemplative wandering the face of the earth, bearing his own silence amid the surrounding noise.

Three months later, in September, Merton sent Nhat Hanh a copy of the introduction he had written for a Vietnamese translation of his book *No Man Is an Island*. The text focused on how war is rooted in our failure to love:

Violence rests on the assumption that the enemy and I are entirely different: the enemy is evil and I am good. The enemy must be destroyed and I must be saved. But love sees things differently. It sees that even the enemy suffers from the same sorrows and limitations that I do. That we both have the same hopes, the same needs, the same aspiration for a peaceful and harmless human life. And that death is the same for both of us. Then love may perhaps show me that my brother is not really my enemy and that war is both his enemy and mine. War is our enemy. Then peace becomes possible. . . .

The principles given in this book are . . . derived from religious wisdom which, in the present case, is Christian. But many of these principles run parallel to the ancient teachings of Buddhism. They are in fact in large part universal truths. They are truths with which, for centuries, man has slowly and with difficulty built a civilized world in the effort to make happiness possible, not merely by making life materially better, but by helping men to understand and live their life more fruitfully.

The key to this understanding is the truth that "No man is an island." A selfish life cannot be fruitful. It cannot be true. It contradicts the very nature of man. The dire effect of this contradiction cannot be avoided: where men live selfishly, in quest of brute power and lust and money, they destroy one another. The only way to change such a world is to change the thoughts and the desires of the men who live in it.

We must believe in the power of love. We must recognize that our being itself is grounded in love: that is to say that we come into being because we are loved and because we are meant to love others. The failure to believe this and to live accordingly creates instead a deep mistrust, a suspicion of others, a hatred of others, and a failure to love. When a man attempts to live by and for himself alone, he becomes a little "island" of hate, greed, suspicion, fear, desire. Then his whole outlook on life is falsified. All his judgments are affected by this untruth. In order to recover the true perspective, which is that of love and compassion, he must once again learn, in simplicity, trust and peace, that "No man is an island."[7]

---

7. HR, 119-26.

Merton sent me a copy of his introduction with this comment:

It was rather an eerie experience a few weeks ago to receive . . . a request to write a preface for the Viet[namese] translation of No Man Is an Island. *The whole thing brings home the futility of so-called spiritual literature in this day and age. Who is going to have time for pious meditations with the whole place getting showered in napalm? Maybe someone in a plush apartment in Saigon. . . . I tried to say something, and to say it non-politically. Don't know if it makes any sense. I was too embarrassed. I guess being embarrassed is a luxury too. Everything is. Life is.*[8]

No doubt Merton's encounter with Nhat Hanh figured in his one piece of writing aimed specifically at Vietnamese readers. Certainly their meeting was one of the preparatory steps for his own journey to Asia. His last letter to me, sent from California on August 5, 1968, four months before his death in Bangkok, included a request for Nhat Hanh's current address.

The madness and mayhem occurring in Vietnam haunted our correspondence throughout 1967 and much of 1968. When the CPF and the Fellowship of Reconciliation began a project to raise funds for medical assistance to civilian war casualties in both South and North Vietnam, Merton drafted a two-page statement making the case for such a campaign:

Most of the war victims in Vietnam are non-combatants. It is estimated that for every enemy combatant killed, five non-combatants are killed, the very people the US declares it is trying to "save." Thousands of women, children and old people have been destroyed, maimed and disfigured by the latest and most destructive weapons our technology has devised.[9]

Merton saw the U.S. strategy of destroying entire villages as "systematic terrorism being used to break the morale of anyone tempted

---

8. HGL, 297-98.
9. NVA, 266.

Napalm exploding in a Vietnamese village.

to resist." Similar tactics, he pointed out, were used by the Nazis in World War II and were at that time universally condemned. He found it a source of scandal that there were church leaders support-ing the war while turning a blind eye to its atrocities. That the human targets of the war were non-white would not go unnoticed by non-white people elsewhere in the world, including in the United States itself. "We need not be surprised if we find fire and violence in our own backyard," Merton noted. "We will simply be getting a very slight taste of our own medicine."

Not only must the war be opposed," Merton wrote, "but every effort must be made "to help the innocent victims." Such assistance gives us "the opportunity to salvage at least a vestige of Christian decency, to show our sorrow for the immense harm that has been done, and to make some kind of reparation to those who have been harmed."

Merton concluded with words Albert Camus had written during the French-Algerian War:

Some people are not aware of the real horror of the situation: these have no business trying to make a judgment of it. Others are aware, but they go on heroically insisting that our brothers must perish rather than our obsessions. Such people I can admire only from a distance.[10]

In *Faith and Violence*, a book dedicated to Phil Berrigan and myself that came into print just after Merton's death, the Vietnam War was a major topic. One of the chapters, "Vietnam—An Overwhelming Atrocity,"[11] was Merton's most vehement statement about the destruction of lives, villages, and entire habitats that was going on in Southeast Asia. Front and center in Merton's view of the war were the women and children, the aged and infirm who were the primary victims of the napalm bombs that fell in regions of Vietnam classified by the U.S. military as "free fire zones" in which anything that moved was a target. For readers who might be unaware of what napalm was, Merton quoted from a report issued by a group of physicians who had worked in Vietnam: "Napalm is a highly sticky inflammable jelly which clings to anything it touches and burns with such heat that all oxygen in the area is exhausted within moments. Death is either by roasting or suffocation.... Those who survive face a living death. The victims are often children."

But, Merton commented, war-promoting propaganda seeks to focus our attention on images that portray the military in benevolent roles:

Pictures of GIs bestowing candy bars on half-naked "native" children are supposed to give us all the information we need ... [the illusion that these] are happy people who love our boys because we are saving them from the Reds and teaching them "democracy." It is of course important for the public to believe this because otherwise the war itself would be questioned, and as a matter of fact it is questioned.

10. The Camus quotation comes from *Actuelles III: Chroniques algériennes, 1939-1958. Avant propos*; translation by Merton.

11. The essay was originally published in the March 1968 issue of *The Catholic Worker*.

Never before in American history was there a war that was so much questioned![12]

Merton contrasted a bland statement made to President Johnson by an unnamed American Catholic bishop[13] that the war was "a sad and heavy obligation imposed by the mandate of love" with the words of a Buddhist nun in Vietnam: "You Americans come to help the Vietnamese people, but have brought only death and destruction."

Her words highlighted, Merton remarked, how American perceptions of Vietnam were utterly divorced from human reality:

The tragic thing about Vietnam is that, after all, the "realism" of our program there is so unrealistic, so rooted in myth, so completely out of touch with the needs of the people whom we know only as statistics and to whom we never manage to listen, except when they fit in with our own psychopathic delusions. Our external violence in Vietnam is rooted in an inner violence which simply ignores the human reality of those whom we claim to be helping.[14]

---

12. FV, 89.
13. In fact it was Archbishop Robert Lucey of San Antonio, Texas.
14. FV, 92.

Merton was also haunted by an awareness of the emptiness of so many words that were being used to justify the war in Vietnam as well as preparations for nuclear war. In one of his last essays, "War and the Crisis of Language,"[15] Merton analyzed the modern corruption of language in which arguments are presented in so tautological a way that dialogue ends before it begins. It is the language of the repeated declaration of slogans and sterilized phrases, a language of advertising, a language without question marks.

A perfect example of such deadening of language was the comment made by an American commander who ordered the aerial destruction of a Vietnamese village: "In order to save the village, it became necessary to destroy it." If innocent villagers were killed, this was an unfortunate but necessary price that the (never consulted) Vietnamese people had to pay for the safeguarding of their "freedom." The "philosophy" of the Pentagon and many supporters of the Vietnam War was hardly different than the plot of a good guy–bad guy western movie:

> If he is a bad guy, he obviously has to be killed. If he is a good guy, he is on our side and he ought to be ready to die for freedom. We will provide an opportunity for him to do so: we will kill him to prevent him falling under the tyranny of a demonic enemy.

The molding of language—"double-talk, tautology, ambiguous cliché, self-righteous and doctrinaire pomposity, and pseudoscientific jargon"—to prevent seeing the catastrophic human reality of war becomes the ultimate mark of absolute power, the power of mass killing in which everyone living in "an enemy zone" is a legitimate target.

---

15. PFP, 300-314. Originally published in *The Critique of War*, ed. Robert Ginsberg (Chicago: Henry Regnery, 1969).

Blessed Are the Meek

PUBLICATION OF THE Catholic Peace Fellowship's booklet edition of Merton's "Blessed Are the Meek," an essay that centered on the Christian roots of nonviolence, was a recurrent topic in our correspondence in 1967. Merton had even gotten his abbot, Dom James Fox, to donate $500 of monastery funds to help the CPF with printing costs.

"Blessed Are the Meek" had been written in January 1966 in response to a request from Hildegard Goss-Mayr, co-secretary of the International Fellowship of Reconciliation in Vienna. In German translation, it had first been published in the journal *Der Christ in der Welt* (Christ in the World).

The CPF booklet was dedicated to folk singer and peace activist Joan Baez. "Joan was down here last December," Merton wrote, "and I had a good talk with her—like her very much. . . ."[1] Merton was pleased that graphic artist Corita Kent had volunteered to design a colorful cover.

Merton's text pointed out that meekness is not a quality many aspire to, in part because the word is often misunderstood. The meekness referred to in the Gospels, he stressed, had nothing to do with weakness or cowardice, nor did it mean those who are by temperament quiet and obedient no matter what is demanded of them:

> Still less does it mean "blessed are they who passively submit to unjust oppression." On the contrary, we know that the "poor in spirit" are those of whom the prophets spoke . . . the "humble of the earth" . . . the oppressed who have no human weapons to rely on and who nevertheless are true to the commandments [of God].[2]

---

1. HGL, 303-304.
2. Merton mailed the finished text to Hildegard on January 14, 1966 with a

For the Christian, Merton explained:

The basis of nonviolence is the Gospel message of salvation for all men and of the Kingdom of God to which all are summoned. The disciple of Christ, he who has heard the good news, the announcement of the Lord's coming and of His victory, and is aware of the definitive establishment of the Kingdom, proves his faith by the gift of his whole self to the Lord in order that all may enter the Kingdom. The great historical event, the coming of the Kingdom, is made clear and is "realized" in proportion as Christians themselves live the life of the Kingdom in the circumstances of their own place and time.... The religious basis of Christian nonviolence is ... faith in Christ the Redeemer and obedience to his demand to love and manifest himself in us by a certain manner of acting in the world and in relation to other men. This obedience enables us to live as true citizens of the Kingdom, in which the divine mercy, the grace, favor and redeeming love of God are active in our lives.... The chief place in which this new mode of life is set forth in detail is the Sermon on the Mount. At the very beginning of this great inaugural discourse, the Lord numbers the beatitudes, which are the theological foundation of Christian nonviolence: Blessed are the poor in spirit ... blessed are the meek.[3]

The early history of the church, Merton noted, provides a remarkable example of the transformative power of nonviolent witness:

The record of the apostles and martyrs remains to testify to this inherent and mysterious dynamism of the ecclesial "event" in the world of history and time. Christian nonviolence is rooted in this consciousness and this faith....

A real understanding of Christian nonviolence (backed up by the evidence of history in the Apostolic Age) shows not only that it is a

---

letter noting that it was a good day to be sending the essay as it was the feast day of Saint Hilary of Poitiers, who said, "The best way to solve the problem of rendering to Caesar what is Caesar's is to have nothing that is Caesar's" (HGL, 337). The full text of "Blessed are the Meek" is in both *Faith and Violence,* 14-39, and *Passion for Peace,* 248-62.

3. Matthew 5:3-4.

*power, but that it remains perhaps the only really effective way of
transforming man and human society. After nearly fifty years of Communist revolution, we find little evidence that the world is improved
by violence.*

Aware how easily reformers wander into the quicksand of self-
righteousness, Merton warned of the danger of idealism:

*Wherever there is a high moral ideal there is an attendant risk of
pharisaism, and nonviolence is no exception. The basis of pharisaism is division: on the one hand this morally or socially privileged self
and the elite to which it belongs. On the other hand, the "others," the
wicked, the unenlightened, whoever they may be. . . . Christian nonviolence . . . is not built on presupposed division, but on the basic unity of
man. It is not out for the conversion of the wicked to the ideas of the
good, but for the healing and reconciliation of man with himself, man
the person and man the human family.*

The nonviolent resister fights not merely for his own private truth
"but for *the* truth, common to him *and* to the adversary. . . . He is
fighting for *everybody*."

*[In obedience to the Gospel, the meek Christian] effaces himself and
his own interests and even risks his life in order to testify not simply
to "the truth" in a sweeping, idealistic and purely platonic sense, but
to the truth that is incarnate in a concrete human situation, involving
living persons whose rights are denied or whose lives are threatened.*

Merton quoted from the address given by Pope Paul VI before
the United Nations General Assembly just a few months earlier,
October 4, 1965. "No more war, war never again," Paul had declared.
"If you wish to be brothers, let the weapons fall from your hands.
You cannot love with offensive weapons in your hands."

Merton saw Christian hope and Christian humility as insepa-
rable:

*The quality of nonviolence is decided largely by the purity of the
Christian hope behind it. In its insistence on certain human values,*

the Second Vatican Council, following Pacem in terris, *displayed a basically optimistic trust in man himself. Not that there is not wickedness in the world, but today trust in God cannot be completely divorced from a certain trust in man. The Christian knows that there are radically sound possibilities in every man, and he believes that love and grace always have the power to bring out those possibilities at the most unexpected moments. Therefore if he has hopes that God will grant peace to the world it is because he also trusts that man, God's creature, is not basically evil: that there is in man a potentiality for peace and order. . . . Despair is not permitted to the meek, the humble, the afflicted, the ones famished for justice, the merciful, the clean of heart and the peacemakers. All the beatitudes "hope against hope," "bear everything, believe everything, hope for everything, endure everything."*[4] *The beatitudes are simply aspects of love.*

In the last section of his essay, Merton reflected on our need to recover a more childlike attitude:

The hope of the Christian must be, like the hope of a child, pure and full of trust. The child is totally available in the present because he has relatively little to remember, his experience of evil is as yet brief, and his anticipation of the future does not extend far. The Christian, in his humility and faith, must be as totally available to his brother, to his world, in the present, as the child is. But he cannot see the world with childlike innocence and simplicity unless his memory is cleared of past evils by forgiveness, and his anticipation of the future is hopefully free of craft and calculation. For this reason, the humility of Christian nonviolence is at once patient and uncalculating. The chief difference between nonviolence and violence is that the latter depends entirely on its own calculations. The former depends entirely on God and on His word.

Merton again addressed the question of genuine, as opposed to cowardly, nonviolence in his essay "Peace and Revolution: A Footnote from *Ulysses*":

---

4. 1 Corinthians 13:7.

Has nonviolence been found wanting? Yes and no. It has been found wanting wherever it has been the nonviolence of the weak. It has not been found so when it has been the nonviolence of the strong. What is the difference? It is a difference of language. The language of spurious nonviolence is merely another, more equivocal form of the language of power. It is a different method of expressing one's will to power. It is used and conceived pragmatically, in reference to the seizure of power. But that is not what nonviolence is about. Nonviolence is not for power but for truth. It is not pragmatic but prophetic. It is not aimed at immediate political results, but at the manifestation of fundamental and crucially important truth. Nonviolence is not primarily the language of efficacy, but the language of kairos [the propitious moment]. *It does not say "We shall overcome" so much as "This is the day of the Lord, and whatever may happen to us,* He *shall overcome." And this, of course, is the dimension that is entirely absent from the Cyclops episode in Ulysses. Unhappily, it is too often absent from our world and our practice today. As a result people begin to imagine that to say "only force works" is to discredit nonviolence. This halftruth—that only force is efficacious—may turn out to be one of the most dangerous illusions of our time. It may do more than anything else to promote an irresponsible and meaningless use of force in a pseudo-revolution that will only consolidate the power of the police state. Never was it more necessary to understand the importance of genuine nonviolence as a power for real change because it is aimed not so much at revolution as at conversion. Unfortunately, mere words about peace, love and civilization have completely lost all power to change anything.* [5]

---

5. NVA, 70-75. The essay was originally published in the Fall–Winter 1968 issue of *Peace,* the journal of the American Pax group.

Joy and Grief

HANGING ON A WALL at the Catholic Worker office on Chrystie Street in the early sixties was a quotation from Léon Bloy: "Joy is the most infallible sign of the presence of God." If Bloy was right, God was very present in Thomas Merton. In fact joy and laughter were a significant element in what he had to say about peacemaking, though his good humor and wit were at times an irritation to some of his brothers in the monastic life, and indeed to the grimmer sort of social activist who shares Bertolt Brecht's view that "he who laughs has not yet heard the terrible tidings."[1]

I suspect Merton's basic joy in life had a great deal to do with his ability to persevere, not only within his monastic community, but also with people like myself who were attempting to be peacemakers. If he sometimes spoke critically about both monks and social radicals, it often was in a way that awakened a smile.

During our last two years of correspondence, while we often soberly discussed practical questions regarding the work of the Catholic Peace Fellowship, or larger issues concerning the state of the world and the church, many of his letters reminded me of Merton's gale-force laughter the day we first met.

One laugh-out-loud letter had to do with a party he had attended a day or two earlier. It concerned his old friend and mentor Dan Walsh, a philosophy professor who, in Merton's Columbia days, had been the first person to point Merton toward the Trappists. In 1960, responding to an invitation from Dom James Fox to help reorganize the abbey's teaching program, Walsh moved to Kentucky, initially staying in the monastery guesthouse where I met him during my

---

1. Bertolt Brecht, "To Those Born Later," part of the *Svendborg Poems* (1939).

first visit with Merton. Subsequently he taught philosophy at Bellar-mine College in Louisville. In 1967 it occurred to the archbishop of Louisville that this modest scholar would make an excellent priest. Merton described the celebration that followed Walsh's ordination.

> [T]here was a lot of celebrating. In fact I celebrated on too much champagne, which is a thing a Trappist rarely gets to do, but I did a very thorough job. At one point in the afternoon I remember looking up and focusing rather uncertainly upon four faces of nuns sitting in a row looking at me in a state of complete scandal and shock. Another pillar of the Church had fallen.[2]

When I sent him a letter typed on a piece of stationery designed by Linda Henry that had the words "the monks are moving" running sideways down the right side of the page, Merton responded with a request for a packet for use with some of his own correspondence, then added:

> Only thing is I wonder if the monks are moving. Everything I do gives me scruples about being identified with this stupid rhinocerotic out-fit that charges backward into the jungle with portentous snuffling and then bursts out of the canebrake with a roar in the most unlikely places.[3]

In a letter remarking on his poorly organized filing system, he wrote:

> It is true, I do have files and I do keep copies of letters. But I can never find anything in the files, and I don't know what happens to the copies of letters. I guess my head is so addled with Zen and Sufism that I have totally lapsed into inefficiency, and am rapidly becoming a backward nation if not a primitive race, a Bushman from the word go, muttering incantations to get the fleas out of my whiskers, a vanishing American who has fallen into the mythical East as into a deep dark hole.[4]

---

2. HGL, 303; letter dated June 17, 1967.
3. HGL, 304; letter dated June 26, 1967.
4. HGL, 299; letter dated February 13, 1967.

(Courtesy Thomas Merton Center)

There was a letter that began with a mysterious Yiddish proverb, all in capitals: "SLEEP FASTER WE NEED THE PILLOWS."[5] (Indeed Merton got very little sleep.)

Another letter included a photo—a view of the Kentucky hills, fold upon fold of receding green under a cloudless blue sky, with a steel skyhook, the kind used in construction for lifting substantial objects, that appeared to descend from heaven itself. Merton noted on the back that it was "the only known photograph of God." His letter explained that his snapshot bore witness to a "supernatural event such as (of course) occurs around here at every moment and even more frequently than that. In between the moments. You have to duck all the time to keep from being brained by a supernatural event."[6]

It was in Merton's laughter—often laughter at himself—that I best understood and measured his seriousness. I discovered the connection that necessarily exists between a capacity for joy and grief. A monk who could see God in a giant skyhook dangling above the Kentucky hills and turn red laughing over the fish-market smell of unwashed feet was the same monk who could expose his heart to

---

5. Unpublished letter to Linda Henry dated April 6, 1968; in the archive of the Thomas Merton Center.

6. HGL, 304; letter dated November 18, 1967.

killing in all its horror, see the intentional ending of someone's life as the ultimate iconoclasm, and find it a religious duty to take an active part in combat against war.

Merton's letters to me were more likely to give rise to a smile than mine to him. Occasionally my correspondence with Merton was confessional. In one letter, I wrote about the spirit of enmity that infected me and many others who were campaigning against the Vietnam War:

> *The peace movement is currently plagued with a "hate LBJ" [President Lyndon Baines Johnson] campaign. "LBJ, LBJ, how many kids did you kill today?" is a chant frequently heard at anti-war rallies. Huge ugly caricatures of the president are carried in parades. Nor do I want to sound self-righteous about the problem, for it afflicts me too. For a while I had a photo of the president at the center of the dartboard that hung on the kitchen wall of our apartment and found it amusing to throw darts at the image. No more. The other night I had a dream about getting on a public bus and discovering LBJ was one of the passengers and that there was an empty seat next to him. I sat down and introduced myself and we got into a conversation about the war. We didn't agree— he said more or less the same kinds of things that I had heard him say at press conferences—but it was a real if troubled human exchange. Then, at his suggestion, we got off the bus and went for a walk in the countryside, at this point saying nothing. Gazing downward, I watched our shoes as we kicked up the golden fall leaves that were thick on the ground. We were both silent, just the sound of our shoes plowing the leaves. At that point I woke up and the dream ended. I got out of bed, my mind momentarily blank, and stepped into the kitchen, where I saw the dartboard. The photo of Johnson looked like it had been sprayed with bullets. I just made it back to the bed, collapsed and wept. I felt like a murderer. So you see I'm not talking about problems others have but my own problem, my own sin.*

Merton responded:

> *You are right, Jim, about all the "hate LBJ" stuff. The thing this Vietnam war is proving is that this whole country is rotten with violence*

*and hate and frustration and this means the peaceniks as much as
anybody else. We just don't know what peace and love mean. The only
ones who have really done anything are Martin Luther King and those
who worked so hard at it in the South—and a few others who have
tried here and there in various ways and for various causes. And now
that is being discredited. Of course Dorothy [Day] is there to remind
us with her unfailing wisdom what it is all about too.*[7]

Also in the confessional vein, I wrote to Merton about the failure
of my first marriage. The marriage was eventually annulled by the
Vatican, but not until many years later. In the meantime my entering
into a second civil marriage distressed Dorothy and led her to consider withdrawing as a sponsor of the CPF. The CPF staff, she said,
should set an example of fidelity to church teaching on marriage. I
didn't disagree, only in my long-standing loneliness was grateful to
be re-married. Yet it was sad indeed that my second marriage did not
enjoy the benefit of a formal Catholic blessing. In fact I sympathized
with Dorothy's views and seriously considered leaving the CPF staff.
Unsure what to do, I asked Merton for guidance. Here are extracts
from his response:

*Your letter about Dorothy's offer to resign as sponsor has waited ten
days for an answer. I want to get to it finally, sorry for the delay. I have
been held up by trips to doctors and by a long visit of an old friend.*[8] . . .

*My first thought was perhaps an ironic one. I was reminded imme-
diately of my own attempt to resign when Roger burned himself up
outside the UN. At that time I think Dorothy was quite angry with me
[for my initial response]. Yet I think the problem of what others interpret as suicide is on a par with the problem of what others interpret
as "immorality." I might say at once that I do not in any way judge
your [current] relationship . . . and I think I take a much more flexible
view of it than Dorothy does, though I am no "underground priest." In
other words I am much more prepared to concede that before God you*

---

7. HGL, 298; letter dated November 16, 1966.

8. Sy Freedgood, Merton's friend from Columbia days, had come for a three-
day visit.

are perhaps doing no real moral wrong. But as I say, God alone knows that, and there will still be many who will judge otherwise.

Dorothy is a person of great integrity and consistency and this hits one between the eyes in the way she sums it up [in her letter to you], hard as it may be. I can see where she is in a sense quite right in demanding a like consistency from others who act as "Catholics" formally and explicitly in the eyes of the whole world. Perhaps it would be desirable for everyone to be as she would desire, and as the traditional Church position would demand. Yet we have to face the fact that this inflexible position is called into question not just by mavericks and radicals: there are enormously serious unsolved questions being debated in the Church, especially in the area of marriage, by the most reputable theologians, and the situation is such first that everyone outside the Church is quite aware of it, and second that it is no longer completely possible and fair to impose the old inflexible (though I think better and truer) position as a matter of strict obligation on everyone without further appeal. . . .

On the other hand, I do agree with her that quite apart from the question of sin, it would be better for the head of the Catholic Peace Fellowship to have made the kind of sacrifice she speaks of, and that a lot of us have to make in one way or another.

Nevertheless, all that having been said, I do not think that it is quite fair of her to make it an either/or. Either you resign or her name drops from the list of sponsors—or you give up [your second marriage]. In the new situation where many might be willing to concede that you were not in the wrong and when scandal is not given (possibly) in the way it once would have been, I don't think it is fully just to be so categorical. . . .

One thing I will say: now I am talking in terms of the traditional and accepted theology which Dorothy herself must accept. If there is some way you can continue living with [your new wife], in which, according to the judgment of a reputable authority—even one with whom Dorothy does not necessarily agree—you are not "in sin" (and here the boundaries may be far wider than Dorothy herself would impose), you preserve every right to maintain your position and she does not have any right to question it, except perhaps insofar as "appearances" may need to be "saved" and there I assume she is no more intolerant than any other normal person.

In other words the Church grants you the right to follow your conscience as formed with the approval of a reputable theological opinion or arbiter. This is not new, this is old. No one can question it. It is of course quite possible that the situation cannot be saved in this way.

If not, I still think Dorothy should regard it more as your own personal business, be content to offer you charitable advice, and stop short of withdrawing her name from the list of sponsors. But that is just my opinion. . . .

So on this practical level it turns out to be one very nice mess. If in the end it were possible for you to consider the thing in terms of sacrifice, this of course would be ideal and admirable. I do not urge this on you, certainly not as an obligation. I only say that in the abstract, and in terms of Catholic tradition and the lives of the saints, this is theoretically "the best." Yet I simply cannot evade the fact that this "best" is very much under fire today from people whom I cannot dismiss as morally irresponsible.

My own monastic vocation is constantly being called into question on these grounds, and if I hold on to it, which I certainly do, it is no longer on the grounds that it is "best" but on more existential grounds: "It may be absurd, I may not understand it, it may look like madness in the eyes of all these cats, but it happens to be what I am called to, and this is what I am going to do."

Ultimately, I think it is on this level that all our decisions have to be made today. What does God ask of me?

So I pray that you may see what God is asking of you, really and truly, and that he may give you the strength to do just that, as best you can. Pray for me too, Jim. I hate to see anyone in such a bind. God love you. Happy Easter. . . . [9]

9. HGL, 301-3; letter dated March 21, 1967. A letter sent by Merton in mid-June added: "I do hope everything is forgotten, with Dorothy and so on. Thinking back to my letter, I realize how inadequate it was and in any case I had only the very vaguest notion of what was happening. I tried to say things that Dorothy would

Merton's letter was an immense help not only to me but to Dorothy, who decided after all to remain a sponsor and even apologized to me for being too judgmental.

Quite a letter, and there were so many. It still astonishes me that Merton found time to write to me year after year, often at length. Of course not all my letters to him were answered—he simply hadn't enough time. In the late sixties one of Merton's solutions to the problem of too much mail was the use of mimeographed circular letters. For example there was a two-page Christmas letter in 1966 that began with an apology about his inability to respond personally to everyone who wrote, but went on to comment on some of the questions correspondents had lately put to him.

To those who were distressed about his opposition to the U.S. role in Vietnam (one correspondent had asked, "Are you going to let the Communists take over everything?"), he argued that the war is so brutal and devastating that it hardly matters who takes over in the end—in fact "the US seems to be driving Asia into the arms of Communism." Merton opposed an either–or mode of thinking, "as if there were only Communism and the US, no other choice." He asked friends to pray for Thich Nhat Hanh, "*persona non grata* with both sides because he favors looking for other alternatives."

Many letters sent to him, he noted, were requests for prayer, with some describing painful inner struggles. One section of his Christmas letter offered this advice:

> *The heart of man can be full of so much pain, even when things are exteriorly "all right." It becomes all the more difficult because today we are used to thinking that there are explanations for everything. But there is no explanation of most of what goes on in our own hearts, and we cannot account for it all. No use resorting to the kind of mental tranquilizers that even religious explanations sometimes offer. Faith must be deeper than that, rooted in the unknown and in the abyss of*

---

have to accept. I hope everything is now fixed up and that you are at peace and that God's blessing is with you both—and that people will mind their own business in the future" (HGL, 303).

darkness that is the ground of our being. No use teasing the darkness to try to make answers grow out of it. But if we learn how to have a deep inner patience, things solve themselves, or God solves them if you prefer: but do not expect to see how. Just learn to wait, and do what you can and help other people. Often it is in helping someone else we find the best way to bear our own trouble.

A personal letter Merton sent to me in January 1967 included some reflections on technology. Reviewing *Conjectures of a Guilty Bystander*, Merton's latest book, one critic had taken Merton to task for being too negative about technology and even making fun of it. This struck a nerve. In his letter Merton commented that he just couldn't buy the utopian view that technology necessarily equals

progress and a better life. In fact "machines do not guarantee that things will be better for the poor worker"—what "new, improved" machines will often mean is not less backbreaking employment "but no employment, period. And no eating also." In any event, he added:

I don't have to be part of anybody's in-group and keep up with the cozy current opinions. . . . [In fact] there is every reason for someone like me to keep on uttering opinions that are a bit divergent and that come from an

(Photo by Jim Forest)

unexpected angle. The secular city[10] *does not need me in it, but out of it looking in.*[11]

Part of his next letter was a continuation of this topic:

I am entitled to the bare recognition that I am not just chanting the slogans of this or that side. . . . I go to considerable effort to think out

---

10. Harvey Cox's book *The Secular City* was a bestseller at the time.
11. Letter dated January 28, 1967; not included in HGL.

my own positions, and to continue thinking them out when they are not satisfactory.... When I say something like "the realm of politics is the realm of waste" I mean precisely the farce we witness every day: appropriating insignificant funds for the "war on poverty" and then taking them back and pouring them into immense sums of money spent on war and destruction, of wiping people out instead of helping them to live.[12]

Still mulling over the modern world's uncritical romance with technology, five days later Merton sent me an article by the independent Washington journalist I. F. Stone (Merton may well have been Stone's only monastic reader) that sounded like it could have been written by Merton himself:

Everything America stands for is at stake [in Vietnam]. And not just America, but everything the modern world admires. And not just the capitalist world, but all that Lenin and his comrades aspired to.... It is the Machine. It is the prestige of the machine that is at stake in Vietnam. It is Boeing and General Electric and Goodyear and General Dynamics. It is the electronic rangefinder and the amphibious truck and the night-piercing radar. It is the defoliant, and the herbicide, and the deodorant.... It is the ideal of our young men ... to be an Ivy-League executive in one of those chrome and glass skyscrapers which are our cathedrals. It is to be a human particle as shiny and antiseptic and replaceable as any machine part, in the world of business. This is more than a drive for money. It is the veneration of efficiency. It is faith in technology.... [13]

Meanwhile a letter received from Merton in June 1967 expressed worries regarding the direction of monastic life at Gethsemani:

The abbot is now away but I get vague storm warnings that when he gets back I am going to be in trouble. Something about the Apostolic Delegate [Vatican diplomat to the United States] objecting to my activities. We'll see. I couldn't care less. Except it is a little stupid being

12. Letter dated February 13, 1967; this portion of the letter was not included in the extracts published in HGL.

13. I. F. Stone, "More Than Steel and Chrome Can Bear," *I. F. Stone's Weekly* 13 (February 1967); www.unz.org/Pub/IFStonesWeekly.

involved in this elaborate organization that constantly trumpets its successes and advances.[14]

His next letter, nine days later, picked up the same thread:

One of our latest one step forward, two steps backward moves: censorship of mail was called off in December [1966] here, and has been called back on again, I understand. Just waiting for the announcement and for the loss of several interesting correspondents.[15]

The rumor was false. In fact quite different changes were afoot that would not only end censorship of mail once and for all but give Merton unimpeded latitude as a writer. In June Merton was at last totally freed from the impediment of censorship when his chief censor, Father Paul Bourn, wrote, "Don't fret about censorship. I've about reached the point where I consider it inappropriate." Not quite believing the good news, Merton continued to send his prose writings to Father Bourn, only to have them returned that the assurance that "the 'green light' was now on permanent."[16]

In September 1967 came even more astonishing news: Dom James Fox was stepping down as abbot and, following Merton's example, would be retiring to a hermitage. It was truly the end of an era at the Abbey of Gethsemani.

Four months later Dom James's successor was elected: Father Flavian Burns,[17] a former student of Merton. It was Flavian who opened the door for Merton to travel, including the trip to Asia.

When I wrote Merton in July 1968, no thought was further from my mind that this was my last letter to him. In it I recalled the theme of our 1964 retreat, "the spiritual roots of protest," and wondered if now the word "revolution" wasn't taking the place of "protest." It was the year of the assassinations of Martin Luther King and Robert Kennedy, of urban riots and uprisings in America and other

---

14. HGL, 303; letter dated June 17, 1967.
15. HGL, 304; letter dated June 26, 1967.
16. See the entry on censorship in the *Thomas Merton Encyclopedia*, 47–49.
17. Flavian Burns declined to use the title "Dom."

1st Photos of Viet Mass Slaying

WEATHER
Snow flurries and
colder today.
High in the upper 30s.
Details on Page 1-C.

THE PLAIN DEALER

FINAL
Stocks & Races
Dow-Jones off 5.21

OHIO'S LARGEST NEWSPAPER

128TH YEAR—NO. 324 • • • • •

CLEVELAND, THURSDAY, NOVEMBER 20, 1969

96 PAGES   10 CENTS

Exclusive

This photograph will shock Americans as it shocked the editors and the staff of The Plain Dealer. It was taken by a young Cleveland area man while serving as a photographer with the U.S. Army in South Vietnam.

It was taken during the attack by American soldiers on the South Vietnamese village My Lai, an attack which has made world headlines in recent days with disclosures of mass killings allegedly at the hands of American soldiers.

This photograph and others on two special pages are the first to be published anywhere of the killings.

This particular picture shows a clump of bodies of South Vietnamese civilians which includes women and children. Why they were killed raises one of the most momentous questions of the war in Vietnam.

Cameraman Saw GIs Slay 100 Villagers

By JOSEPH ESZTERHAS
(c) 1969, The Plain Dealer

A clump of bodies on a road in South Vietnam.

Newspaper headline about My Lai massacre.

parts of the world, of slums on fire, of the My Lai massacre in Vietnam, of draft-record burning in Maryland, and of major cultural shifts. Revolution was being talked about and advocated by many. Was Merton himself pointing in that direction, I asked, in speaking about the basic inadequacies of political means in bringing fundamental changes?

Not at all, he replied:

I hear a lot of political talk about revolution coming in and it sounds highly irresponsible and calculated to do nothing but get a lot of people's heads knocked off for no purpose whatever. More and more I see the thing in terms of a kind of post-political eschatology which in any case I cannot articulate. Of course I know this would be most unacceptable to the people who are convinced they can get somewhere with direct action. To just up and say we are under God's judgment [as

I do], well, I guess that doesn't cut ice with anyone. However, that's where we are. And maybe we're going to find out something about it.[18]

His letter reminded me that the only revolution that Merton found worth pursuing was a nonviolent revolution of the heart.

A few weeks later, in September, I received my last note from Merton. On his way to Asia, he visited a small Trappist monastery of women at Redwoods in northern California, and from there sent me a postcard with a three-sentence message:

We are at the meeting at Redwoods in an atmosphere of love and peace. Thinking of you and praying for you. Pray for me.[19]

"Pray for me" were the final words of a seven-year correspondence.

In my biography of Merton, *Living with Wisdom,* I wrote in detail about his Asian journey and Merton's death. In this book let me opt for brevity.

Merton flew to the Far East in mid-October. In the course of eight weeks he visited India, Sri Lanka, and Thailand, spoke at an interreligious conference in Calcutta, and had conversations with several Tibetan Buddhist monks, including a dialog with the Dalai Lama that was spread over four days.[20] On December 10, after delivering a lecture at a conference near Bangkok of Trappist and Benedictine monks, he died of accidental electrocution after taking a shower. He was fifty-three. The day after his death, his body was taken to the U.S. Air Force Base in Bangkok and from there flown back to the United States in the company of bodies of young Americans killed in Vietnam. His grave at the Abbey of Our Lady of Gethsemani has become a place of pilgrimage.

The spirit of Merton's Asian pilgrimage is suggested in these few sentences that ended a lecture he delivered in Calcutta on October 24:

---

18. HGL, 307-308; letter dated August 5, 1968.

19. HGL, 308; undated postcard sent in September 1968.

20. "It was Merton who introduced me to the real meaning of the word 'Christian,'" the Dalai Lama has since said. See *Freedom in Exile: The Autobiography of the Dalai Lama* (New York: HarperCollins, 1990), 189.

The deepest level of communication is not communication, but communion. It is wordless. It is beyond words, and it is beyond speech, and it is beyond concept. Not that we discover a new unity. We discover an older unity. My dear brothers, we are already one. But we imagine that we are not. What we have to recover is our original unity. What we have to be is what we are.[21]

Thomas Merton's grave.

---

21. *The Asian Journal of Thomas Merton* (AJ), 308.

Letter to a Young Activist

EARLY IN 1966 I WAS HARD hit by all sorts of troubles, from Roger LaPorte's death by fire to the disintegration of my first marriage. I was also discouraged about the work I was doing. Despite the fact that opposition to the war was steadily growing, week by week the war was getting worse—troop numbers rising, more and more bombs falling, and ever more casualties, the great majority of which were civilian. "Napalm"—a bomb-delivered, jelly-like substance that clung to bodies like glue while it burned—was a new word in many people's vocabularies. Pictures were being shown on TV of American soldiers using cigarette lighters to burn peasant homes. An Air Force general, Curtis LeMay, had recommended "bombing Vietnam back to the Stone Age." There was even talk of taking "decisive action," that is using nuclear weapons.

It was against this background that, on February 15, I wrote an anguished letter to Merton:

> *Valentine's Day has passed but no let up to the war in Vietnam. Love continues to find a different sort of expression there. Perhaps it is especially suitable that the* Times *this morning carries a story which has as it headline: "Vietnamese Peasants Are Victims of War."*
>
> *I confess to you that I am in a rather bleak mood. . . . For one thing, I am exhausted with ideological discussions. Earlier today I began to type out a few thoughts on your paper concerning protest. I was going to say that I think such words as "pacifist" ought to be forever thrown into the trash basket and that indeed we ought to try to find a new vocabulary for getting across our ideas to the public. But the question comes up, as I work on such a response, Who is listening? Yes, you, for one—you will read my comments, and perhaps in some way they will alter your thoughts on some subject, or strengthen them. Perhaps it will*

even inspire you to write something. Yet even if you do, who is listening? Your words will be dutifully noted by some ... those Christians who care about baptism and membership in the Body of Christ may be influenced by your meditations. But meanwhile murder goes on without interruption. This appalls me to such a degree that I get weary writing it down. Bomb after bomb after bomb slides away from the bomb bays. For every sentence in this letter, a dozen innocents will have died today in Vietnam. The end of the war is beyond imagination.

This morning I wrote a letter to the editor of [a popular Catholic monthly magazine] in which I explained why a recent editorial ... attacking the CPF's Vietnam declaration was poorly reasoned and didn't come to terms with the reality of the situation in Vietnam. ... I felt like a man in Germany in the 1930s trying to explain why Jews ought not to be sent to the concentration camps.

It all seems so utterly clear. You do not murder. You do not kill the innocent. You do not treat people like blemishes on the landscape, or communities as parcels of real estate, or nations as squares on a chessboard.

Yet no group seems more distant from these facts than Christian (and Catholic) Americans. I have all but given up talking to Catholic audiences about Christ; I simply talk about justice, raw basic justice. I think I've come to understand why natural law made its way into our Church. It was simply an attempt to ask us to be, if not holy, then just. At least that.

How is it that we have become so insensitive to human life, to the wonders of this world we live in, to the mystery within us and around us?

And what can we do? What can be done? Who can we become that we are not? What can we undertake that we haven't?

I do not wish to sound despairing. I have by no means given up on this work of ours. But truly I feel like an ant climbing a cliff, and even worse, for in the distance there seems to be the roar of an avalanche. There is no exit, so I will not bother to look for one. I will continue to work, and there are the saving moments, the saving friendships, the artists, there is in fact the faith.

But I write this thinking perhaps you will have some thoughts which might help. But don't feel you have to have any. I don't wish to treat you as a spiritual irrigation system. But your insights have helped me gain perspective at past times.[1]

Merton's reply was the most helpful letter I've ever received:

Dear Jim,

Thanks for the letter and for the awful, and illuminating, enclosure [about the civilian casualties in Vietnam]. I can well understand your sense of desperation. And the "bleak mood." And also I am glad that you wrote about it. As you say, there are no clear answers, and you can guess that I don't have magic solutions for bleak moods: if I did I would use them on my own which are habitually pretty bleak too. But that is just part of this particular life and I don't expect much else.

Actually, I would say one thing that probably accounts for your feelings, besides all the objective and obvious reasons, you are doubtless tired. I don't know whether you are physically tired or not but you have certainly been pouring your emotional and psychic energy into the CPF and all that it stands for, and you have been sustained by hopes that are now giving out. Hence the reaction. Well, the first thing is that you have to go through this kind of reaction periodically, learn to expect it and cope with it when it comes, don't do things that precipitate it, without necessity (you will always have to).

And then this: do not depend on the hope of results. When you are doing the sort of work you have taken on, essentially an apostolic work, you may have to face the fact that your work will be apparently worthless and even achieve no result at all, if not perhaps results opposite to what you expect. As you get used to this idea you start more and more to concentrate not on the results but on the value, the rightness, the truth of the work itself. And there too a great deal has to be gone through, as gradually you struggle less and less for an idea and more and more for specific people. The range tends to narrow down, but it

---

1. My letter is in the Thomas Merton Center archives in Louisville.

gets much more real. In the end, as you yourself mention in passing, it is the reality of personal relationships that saves everything.

You are fed up with words, and I don't blame you. I am nauseated by them sometimes. I am also, to tell the truth, nauseated with ideals and with causes. This sounds like heresy, but I think you will understand what I mean. It is so easy to get engrossed with ideas and slogans and myths that in the end one is left holding the bag, empty, with no trace of meaning left in it. And then the temptation is to yell louder than ever in order to make the meaning be there again by magic. Going through this kind of reaction helps you to guard against this. Your system is complaining of too much verbalizing, and it is right.

This country is SICK, man. It is one of the sickest things that has happened. People are fed on myths, they are stuffed up to the eyes with illusions. They CAN'T think straight. They have a modicum of good will, and some of them have a whole lot of it, but with the mental bombardment everybody lives under, it is just not possible to see straight, no matter where you are looking. The average everyday "Catlick" is probably in worse shape than a lot of others. He has in his head a few principles of faith which lend no coherence whatever to his life. No one has ever sought any coherence from him or given him the idea that he needed any. All he has been asked to do has been to measure up to a few simple notions about sexual morality (which he may or may not quite make, but anyway he knows where he stands—or falls on his face) and he has been taught that the cross and sacrifice in his life mean in practice going off to war every twenty years or so. He has done this with exemplary, unquestioning generosity, and has reaped the results: a corresponding brutalization, which is not his fault and which he thinks has something to do with being a real human being. In this whole area of war and peace, no matter what the Council may have said about it, the average layman and the average priest are all alike conditioned by this mentality. Furthermore, when it is a question of a kind of remote box score of casualties which gives meaning to life each day, they no longer think of the casualties as people—it is just a score. Also they don't want to think of them as people, they want casualties, they want somebody to get it, because they have been brutalized *and this is a fully legitimate way of indulging the brutality that has been engendered in them. It is not only for country, it is even for God.*

You can be as indignant as you like about this: and it is sickening, but being indignant has its disadvantages. It gets you into the same damn-fool game. Take the myth of "getting results." What is the driving power behind the massive stupidity in Vietnam, with its huge expense and its absurd effects? It is the obsession of the American mind with the myth of know-how, and with the capacity to be omnipotent. Once this is questioned, we will go to any lengths, ANY lengths to resolve the doubt that has thus been raised in our minds. The whole cockeyed American myth is at stake in Vietnam and what is happening to it is obvious, it is tearing itself into little shreds and the nation is half nuts in consequence. The national identity is going slowly down the drain in Vietnam and a lot of terrible things are happening in the process. We are learning how bestial and how incredible are the real components of that myth. Vietnam is the psychoanalysis of the US. I wonder if the nation can come out of it and survive. I have a hunch we might be able to. But your stresses and strains, mine, Dan Berrigan's, all of them, are all part of this same syndrome, and it is extremely irritating and disturbing to find oneself, like it or not, involved in the national madness. The fact that you and I and our type have a special answer which runs counter to that of the majority seems at first to make us sane, but does it really? Does it save us from being part of the same damn mess? Obviously not. Theoretically we understand that, but in fact our hearts will not admit it, and we are trying to prove to ourselves that (a) we at least are sane decent people, (b) sanity and decency are such that our sanity and decency ought to influence everybody else. And there is something to this, I am not preaching a complete anomie. Yet the others think the same way about themselves.

In a word, you have said a lot of good things, you have got a lot of ideas across, it has perhaps caused some good reactions among the bad and what has it achieved in terms of the whole national picture: precious little. The CPF is not going to stop the war in Vietnam, and it is not even going to cause very many Catholics to think differently about war and peace. It is simply going to become another image among images in the minds of most Catholics, something around which are centered some vague emotional reactions, for or against. Nevertheless, you will probably, if you continue as you do, begin the laborious job of changing the national mind and opening up the national conscience. How far will you get? God alone knows. All that you and I can ever hope for in terms of visible results is that we will have perhaps contributed something to a clarification of Christian truth in this society, and as a result a few people may have got straight about some things and opened up to the grace of God and made some sense out of their lives, helping a few more to do the same. As for the big results, these are not in your hands or mine, but they can suddenly happen, and we can share in them: but there is no point in building our lives on this personal satisfaction, which may be denied us and which after all is not that important.

So the next step in the process is for you to see that your own thinking about what you are doing is crucially important. You are probably striving to build yourself an identity in your work and your witness. You are using it so to speak to protect yourself against nothingness, annihilation. That is not the right use of your work. All the good that you will do will come not from you but from the fact that you have allowed yourself, in the obedience of faith, to be used by God's love. Think of this more and gradually you will be free from the need to prove yourself, and you can be more open to the power that will work through you without your knowing it.

The great thing after all is to live, not to pour out your life in the service of a myth: and we turn the best things into myths. If you can get free from the domination of causes and just serve Christ's truth, you will be able to do more and will be less crushed by the inevitable disappointments. Because I see nothing whatever in sight but much disappointment, frustration, and confusion. I hope we can avoid a world war: but do we deserve to? I am not thinking so much of ourselves and this country but of all the people who would be killed who never heard of New York and of the USA even, perhaps. It is a pity that they should have to pay for our stupidity and our sins.

The real hope, then, is not in something we think we can do, but in God who is making something good out of it in some way we cannot see. If we can do His will, we will be helping in this process. But we will not necessarily know all about it beforehand. . . .

Returning to the idea of pacifism: I think the word is useless for our purposes. It does not in the least describe what CPF is trying to do, it seems to me, and only gives a false impression. To speak of pacifism today gives people an excuse for bellicism [war as a way of life]: it implies that there is an alternative. One can be a pacifist or a bellicist. But there is no alternative, and it is not a question of some ethical ideal or some cause, but as you say of the plain, basic human justice, the old natural law. . . .

Enough of this. I wanted to answer your letter and I probably over-did the job. But it is at least a gesture, and if it is of no use it shows I would like to be of some use if I could. I will certainly keep you and Tom in my prayers.

All the best . . . in Christ,

Tom[2]

I shared Merton's letter with Tom Cornell and a few other close friends. From time to time, when the sky was turning starless black, I reread it. Twelve years later, a decade after Merton's death, I included much of it in an essay I wrote on Merton's struggles with peacemaking for a chapter in *Thomas Merton: Prophet in the Belly of a Paradox*, a book edited by Gerald Twomey.[3] There it caught the eye of Robert Ellsberg, then managing editor of *The Catholic Worker*, who skillfully trimmed it in such a way that it became "Letter to a Young Activist," the title the abbreviated version has ever since retained. In the years following, "Letter to a Young Activist" has often been reprinted and translated, even made into posters, bookmarks and greeting cards.

---

2. Letter dated February 21, 1966; full text in HGL, 294-97.

3. *Thomas Merton: Prophet in the Belly of a Paradox*, ed. Gerald Twomey (New York: Paulist Press, 1978).

"Letter to a Young Activist" captures the heart of Merton's advice to anyone in a similar burned-out state while eliminating portions that were more directed at me personally and the work of the Catholic Peace Fellowship as it entered its second year. Here in italics is "Letter to a Young Activist" as published in *The Catholic Worker,* interspersed with my own commentary:

Do not depend on the hope of results.

What a challenge that is. Any action one embarks on is undertaken with the hope of positive, tangible results. One *must* have hope that what you do will have an impact. But to the extent you *depend* on success, your capacity to persevere is undermined.

When you are doing the sort of work you have taken on, essentially an apostolic work, you may have to face the fact that your work will be apparently worthless and even achieve no result at all, if not perhaps results opposite to what you expect.

Before receiving Merton's letter it had never occurred to me that peace work is of its nature an apostolic work—quite a dignity but also quite a responsibility. It was not an altogether comforting linkage. Few if any of Christ's apostles died of old age. All of them experienced a great deal of failure and ridicule.

As you get used to this idea, you start more and more to concentrate not on the results but on the value, the rightness, the truth of the work itself.

It's not easy getting used to the idea that what you are doing is probably going to crash against a stone wall. The shift from focusing not on quickly measurable results but rather on the value, rightness, and truth of the work one is doing requires a major shift of perception.

And there too a great deal has to be gone through, as gradually you struggle less and less for an idea and more and more for specific people. The range tends to narrow down, but it gets much more real. In the end, it is the reality of personal relationships that saves everything.

That last sentence became for me one of the most important insights that I ever received from Merton: *"In the end, it is the reality of personal relationships that saves everything."* I know it by heart and recite it often. It sums up incarnational theology. Words and slogans and theories are not nearly as important as how we see and relate to one another—the relationships we build—and not only with friends but with adversaries. In the context of peace work, it suggests getting to know, as best we can, the people and cultures being targeted by our weapons.

> *You are fed up with words, and I don't blame you. I am nauseated by them sometimes. I am also, to tell the truth, nauseated by ideals and with causes. This sounds like heresy, but I think you will understand what I mean. It is so easy to get engrossed with ideas and slogans and myths that in the end one is left holding the bag, empty, with no trace of meaning left in it. And then the temptation is to yell louder than ever in order to make the meaning be there again by magic. Going through this kind of reaction helps you to guard against this. Your system is complaining of too much verbalizing, and it is right.*

Social movements require words and often use slogans to sum up goals. These have their place but it's secondary. In a talk to his novices, Merton—best known for his words—once said, "He who follows words is destroyed." Like arrows, words point but they are not the target. One of Merton's main contributions to many people who were involved in peace efforts was the witness given by his contemplative monastic life in which prayer and meditation were integral elements of every activity, each day having a liturgical and sacramental foundation. What he had to say helped reveal what couldn't be said.

> *The big results are not in your hands or mine, but they suddenly happen, and we can share in them; but there is no point in building our lives on this personal satisfaction, which may be denied us and which after all is not that important.*

I found these few words—"after all [personal satisfaction] is not that important"—especially helpful. It's not important that we personally get to see the results of our efforts, however worthy our goals may be. Here Merton suggests what I have come to think of as a cathedral builder's mentality, a metaphor that easily comes to mind as I live just a minute's walk from a cathedral whose construction began in 1470 and which wasn't completed until fifty years later. By cathedral building standards, half-a-century was fast work—Notre Dame in Paris took nearly two centuries. But even in cases in which construction took less than a century, those who helped lay the foundations of a great cathedral knew they had slight chance of living to see their building roofed. Perhaps they imagined their grandchildren or great-grandchildren having that satisfaction.

The next step in the process is for you to see that your own thinking about what you are doing is crucially important. You are probably striving to build yourself an identity in your work, out of your work and your witness. You are using it, so to speak, to protect yourself against nothingness, annihilation. That is not the right use of your work. All the good that you will do will come not from you but from the fact that you have allowed yourself, in the obedience of faith, to be used by God's love. Think of this more, and gradually you will be free from the need to prove yourself, and you can be more open to the power that will work through you without your knowing it.

Building an identity in one's work is so basic an element for all of us living in a career-driven, results-oriented, fear-wired society that it's hard to imagine another way of identifying ourselves. Asked who we are, we tend to respond with information about what we do. It's not easy to think in other terms, and indeed any more basic answer (what would that be?) might be embarrassing. But if what you do is rooted in attempting to follow Christ, in trying to live a life in which hospitality and love of neighbor is a major element, a life nourished by the eucharist, that foundation may not only keep you going in dark times but actually, ironically, make your work more effective.

The great thing after all is to live, not to pour out your life in the service of a myth: and we turn the best things into myths.

Merton meant myth in the sense of a purely fictitious narrative. In my own case the problem was not so much making myself the servant of a myth (truth often comes wrapped in myth) but the servant of an ideology. Even Christianity can be flattened into an ideology— a loveless closed system of ideas, theories, and concepts, every spark of paschal fire smothered in ashes.

> *If you can get free from the domination of causes and just serve Christ's truth, you will be able to do more and will be less crushed by the inevitable disappointments. Because I see nothing whatever in sight but much disappointment, frustration and confusion.*

It is after all Christ's truth that matters, a truth we experience from time to time but which can never be adequately expressed in words or be obtained by movements and causes. Trying to live within Christ's truth certainly doesn't mean we will live an undented life, a life free of disappointments—there is a reason that Christianity's main symbol is the cross—but it may help prevent frustration and disappointment from becoming despair.

> *The real hope, then, is not in something we think we can do but in God who is making something good out of it in some way we cannot see. If we can do His will, we will be helping in this process. But we will not necessarily know all about it beforehand.*

Thank you, Thomas Merton.

A Square in a Patchwork Quilt

In these pages I have concentrated especially on Merton's writings on war and peace and his often difficult struggle to communicate his reflections on these topics to the reading public. But there is the danger that a book with a narrow focus will fail to show the ways in which one square in a patchwork quilt connects to the quilt as a whole.

For Merton, his efforts to prevent nuclear war and to encourage nonviolent approaches to conflict resolution were not matters that stood apart from his monastic identity but were an integral part of it. To be a monk was, for Merton, a far more profound endeavor than wearing monastic garments, attending Mass each morning, and praying at established times during the day. It is the intrinsic nature of monastic life to bear a particular witness to the kingdom of God, one aspect of which is to be aware of the world beyond the monastery's borders and to raise, when needed, a cautionary, even prophetic, voice. As Merton put it in a letter to me:

> The validity of the Church depends precisely on spiritual renewal, uninterrupted, continuous, and deep. Obviously this renewal is to be expressed in the historical context, and will call for a real spiritual understanding of historical crises, an evaluation of them in terms of their inner significance and in terms of man's growth and the advancement of truth in man's world: in other words, the establishment of the "kingdom of God." The monk is the one supposedly attuned to the inner spiritual dimension of things. If he hears nothing, and says nothing, then the renewal as a whole will be in danger and may be completely sterilized. [1]

---

1. TM to JF, April 29, 1962; HGL 269.

A large part of spiritual life is listening. Every monk at the Abbey of Gethsemani heard not only the sound of the wind, rain, birds, bells, and chant but the noise and vibrations of artillery practice at nearby Fort Knox which regularly shook the territory of Gethsemani, though perhaps few were so attentive as Merton to the implications of all those tremors and distant explosions. In one of many Fort Knox–related journal entries, Merton notes:

> *The guns were pounding at Fort Knox while I was making my afternoon meditation, and I thought that after all this is no mere "distraction," and that I am here because they are there so that, indeed, I am supposed to hear them. They form part of an ever renewed "decision" and commitment for peace.*[2]

It was impossible for Merton not to think what such intrusive noises were all about and the desolate future they were aiming toward. The price of being alert to nature's pleasant sounds was to be equally aware of noises that signaled destruction. As a writer, Merton could not celebrate the former and be silent about the latter.

---

2. Journal entry 22 Dec 1964; DWL, 182.

In 1941 Merton had been attracted to monastic life as with the force of gravity. *The Seven Storey Mountain* presents Merton in a state of profound, uncritical gratitude for having found his spiritual home at the Abbey of Gethsemani. As the years passed, however, he was haunted by the question: *Is this it? And just what is a monk?* Partly this was due to his gradually unfolding sense that monastic practice among Trappists was less than ideal, in some ways even hostile to contemplative life. One of Merton's long-term projects at Gethsemani was to search out and study earlier models of monastic life. After all, as he put it in one essay, if you wished to take a drink of water from the Mississippi, would you prefer doing so in the muddy delta below New Orleans or at the river's transparent headwaters in Minnesota?[3] Best to take one's thirst upstream to the source.

In the 1940s, in his early years as a monk, Merton undertook a careful reading of Saint Bernard of Clairvaux, the twelfth-century founder of the Cistercian Order, of which the Trappists were a seventeenth-century reformist offshoot, with both Cistercians and Trappists being branches of the ancient Benedictine tree. Merton concluded that the Trappist reform had put too much stress on manual labor and failed to preserve monasticism's contemplative core.[4]

Digging deeper, in the 1950s Merton began exploring monasticism's earliest roots. In the introductory essay to a collection of sayings of the first Christian monks, *The Wisdom of the Desert*, Merton stressed the apparent irony of monasticism emerging in the fourth century, precisely when the emperor Constantine had become patron and guardian of Christianity. At last it was safe to be a Christian—the age of martyrdom was over. Yet suddenly there were hundreds and then thousands of Christians taking distance from the urban centers of imperial power, fleeing to caves and huts in remote and arid places in Egypt and Palestine better suited to snakes and scorpions than to human occupation. Merton saw the first monks as passengers leaping overboard from a sinking ship and swimming for their lives. He commented:

---

3. "Prologue to Cassian," in *Cassian and the Fathers* (CF), 5.
4. See the entry on monasticism in *The Thomas Merton Encyclopedia*, 300-303.

[The first monks] believed that to let oneself drift along, passively accepting the tenets and values of what they knew as society, was purely and simply a disaster. The fact that the Emperor was now Christian and that the world was coming to know the Cross as a symbol of temporal power only strengthened them in their resolve. . . . These men seem to have thought . . . that there is no such thing as a "Christian state."[5]

It had been in just such a state that the 26-year-old Merton had rung the bell of the gatehouse door at the Abbey of Gethsemani.

The monastic exodus from mainstream society, then and now, might seem at first antisocial, yet Merton insisted such monks were not merely rebels against society:

True, they were in a certain sense "anarchists," and it will do no harm to think of them in that light. They were men who did not believe in letting themselves be passively guided and ruled by a decadent state, and who believed that there was a way of getting along without slavish dependence on accepted, conventional values. But they did not place themselves above society.

In a talk Merton gave at a conference near Bangkok on the day he died, he stressed the monk's prophetic role: "The monk is essentially someone who takes a critical attitude toward the contemporary world and its structures."[6] Indeed the monastery provides an excellent vantage point from which to see the world as it is and to read the signs of the times. The monk has the advantage of being relatively free of the constant barrage of propaganda, often disguised as news, with which most of us are inundated.

One gets a glimpse of Merton's mature understanding of his monastic calling in letters he sent in 1967 to Rosemary Radford Ruether, then a young Catholic theologian teaching in Washington, DC. Ruether had challenged Merton to leave the monastery, with its "moribund structures," and encounter Christ "in the steaming ghetto

---

5. WD, 4-5.

6. AJ, 329.

of the big city."[7] In his reply to Ruether's indictment of monasticism, Merton rejected the view that the monastery was an escape hatch and the idea that monks regard themselves as having embraced a higher, more perfect form of Christianity. Merton saw monasticism as a particular form of Christian life, neither higher nor lower than others, that serves basic needs of both church and society. "I honestly believe," Merton wrote, "that this is the right place for me . . . insofar as it's the right battlefield. . . . I would be leading a less honest and more faked life if I were back in the cities. . . . In staying here I am not just being here for myself alone but for my friends, my Church, and all those I am one with. . . . As far as I can see I am a tramp and not much else. But this kind of tramp is what I am supposed to be."[8]

It was the nature of a contemplative vocation, Merton was certain, not to be a "mass man," someone manufactured on society's—or the church's—assembly line, someone whose main choices were shaped by fear or social pressure. Whether under monastic vows or not, the contemplative faces the lonely quest of finding one's "true face." This is the main theme of one of Merton's best essays, "Rain and the Rhinoceros." It's an essay that has its own background sound, a downpour of rain:

> *I came up here from the monastery last night, sloshing through the cornfield, said Vespers, and put some oatmeal on the Coleman stove for supper. It boiled over while I was listening to the rain and toasting a piece of bread at the log fire. The night became very dark. The rain surrounded the whole cabin with its enormous virginal myth, a whole world of meaning, of secrecy, of silence, of rumor. Think of it: all that speech pouring down, selling nothing, judging nobody, drenching the thick mulch of dead leaves, soaking the trees, filling the gullies and crannies of the wood with water, washing out the places where men have stripped the hillside! What a thing it is to sit absolutely alone, in the forest, at night, cherished by this wonderful, unintelligible,*

---

7. *At Home in the World: The Letters of Thomas Merton and Rosemary Radford Ruether* (AHW), 20.

8. Ibid, 23-24.

Merton's hermitage. (Photo by Michael Plekhon)

perfectly innocent speech, the most comforting speech in the world, the talk that rain makes by itself all over the ridges, and the talk of the watercourses everywhere in the hollows! Nobody started it, nobody is going to stop it. It will talk as long as it wants, this rain. As long as it talks I am going to listen.[9]

One of the essay's key words is "fun." Merton found it on the box his Coleman lantern had come packaged in—it was a lantern that "stretches days to give more hours of fun." Merton protested:

There are always a few people who are in the woods at night, in the rain (because if there were not the world would have ended), and I am one of them. We are not having fun, we are not "having" anything, we are not "stretching our days," and if we had fun it would not be measured by hours. Though as a matter of fact that is what fun seems to be: a state of diffuse excitation that can be measured by the clock and "stretched" by an appliance. There is no clock that can measure the speech of this rain that falls all night on the drowned and lonely forest.[10]

---

9. RU, 9-10.
10. RU, 13-14.

At this point, stirred by the ominous noise of a nuclear-armed B52 Strategic Air Command bomber passing overhead, Merton is made aware of the time and and perhaps glances at the clock:

Of course at three-thirty A.M. the SAC plane goes over, red light winking low under the clouds, skimming the wooded summits on the south side of the valley, loaded with strong medicine. Very strong. Strong enough to burn up all these woods and stretch our hours of fun into eternities.

A lone man listening to noises most of us sleep through. The root meaning of the word "monk" is the Greek word *monokos*—a person who is alone, a solitary. One does not have to belong to a monastery to experience and benefit from inner solitude. In his rain-drenched essay, Merton stresses the positive significance of being alone:

One who is not "alone" . . . has not discovered his identity. He seems to be alone, perhaps, for he experiences himself as "individual." But because he is willingly enclosed and limited by the laws and illusions of collective existence, he has no more identity than an unborn child in the womb. He is not yet conscious. He is alien to his own truth. He has senses, but he cannot use them. He has life, but not identity. To have an identity, he has to be awake, and aware. But to be awake, he has to accept vulnerability and death. Not for their own sake: not out of stoicism or despair—only for the sake of the invulnerable inner reality which we cannot recognize (which we can only be) but to which we awaken only when we see the unreality of our vulnerable shell. The discovery of this inner self is an act and affirmation of solitude.

Now if we take our vulnerable shell to be our true identity, if we think our mask is our true face, we will protect it with fabrications even at the cost of violating our own truth. This seems to be the collective endeavor of society: the more busily men dedicate themselves to it, the more certainly it becomes a collective illusion, until in the end we have the enormous, obsessive, uncontrollable dynamic of fabrications designed to protect mere fictitious identities—"selves," that is to say, regarded as objects. Selves that can stand back and see themselves having fun (an illusion which reassures them that they are real).[11]

All things have their season, Merton writes. There is a time for each of us to remain unborn, to be enclosed in the social womb with its warmth and collective myths, but freedom comes only following exodus from the collective womb:

> *He who is spiritually "born" into a mature identity is liberated from the enclosing womb of myth and prejudice. He learns to think for himself, guided no longer by the dictates of need and by the systems and processes designed to create artificial needs and then "satisfy" them.*[12]

The emancipation that follows birth from the societal womb, Merton comments, can take two basic forms. The first is the active life, "which liberates itself from enslavement to necessity by considering and serving the needs of others, without thought of personal interest or return."

The second—Merton's own path—was the contemplative life:

> *[The contemplative life] must not be construed as an escape from time and matter, from social responsibility and from the life of sense, but rather as an advance into solitude and the desert, a confrontation with poverty and the void, a renunciation of the empirical self, in the presence of death and nothingness, in order to overcome the ignorance and error that spring from the fear of "being nothing." The man who dares to be alone can come to see that the "emptiness" and "usefulness" which the collective mind fears and condemns are necessary conditions for the encounter with truth.*[13]

Whichever path one follows, to fail to leave the social womb is to become a mass man. But escaping from the culture of mass men is dangerous. Here Merton turns to *Rhinoceros*, a play by Eugene Ionesco.[14] In it the central figure discovers he no longer resembles

---

11. RU, 14-15.
12. RU, 17.
13. RU, 17-18.
14. A video of the play can be seen on YouTube: www.youtube.com.

anyone—he is the one human left in a world in which everyone else has become part of a vast herd of rhinoceroses—in Merton's vocabulary, a prisoner of the social womb. From the point of view of the rhinoceros, Merton remarks, it is the lone man who is a monster.

Merton comments that Ionesco's play is not merely against conformism but is about totalitarianism. "The rhinoceros is not an amiable beast."

Merton's essay ends with the last raindrop:

> *The rain has stopped. The afternoon sun slants through the pine trees. . . . A dandelion, long out of season, has pushed itself into bloom between the smashed leaves of last summer's day lilies. The valley resounds with the totally uninformative talk of creeks and wild water. . . . Yet even here the earth shakes. Over at Fort Knox the Rhinoceros is having fun.*[15]

---

15. RU, 23.

The Root of Sin Is Fear

IN HIS SPEECH BEFORE THE U.S. CONGRESS, Pope Francis described Thomas Merton as "above all a man of prayer, a thinker who challenged the certitudes of his time and opened new horizons for souls and for the Church. He was also a man of dialogue, a promoter of peace between peoples and religions." Merton was notable, the pope added, for "his openness to God."

Perhaps it was Merton's openness to God that was the driving force behind his qualities as a man of prayer, as a thinker, as someone opening new horizons, as a man of dialogue, as a promoter of peace, and—to make one addition to Francis's list—a monk challenging the rule of fear.

Few sentences have helped me so much and so often as the six words from Merton which serve as the title of this book: *"The root of war is fear."* In fact, fear is the root cause not only of war but of innumerable damaging structures, bad choices, and calamitous actions. One could say, "The root of sin is fear."

Fear is a powerful emotion that has the potential of taking over our lives even when there is no rational threat. A classic example: On October 30, 1938, during a radio dramatization of H. G. Wells's novel *War of the Worlds*, many listeners, mistaking what they heard for a genuine news broadcast, became convinced that Earth was being invaded by Martians. As one newspaper put it, a "tidal wave of terror swept the nation." There were listeners who fled their homes in panic.[1]

Of course there are countless sensible reasons for being fearful: the threat of crime, attack, war, illness, injury, job loss, destitution, homelessness. . . . The list is as long as you care to make it. Such anxieties deserve sober attentiveness without becoming the mainspring

---

1. Barry Glassner, *The Culture of Fear* (New York: Basic Books, 1999), 205-6.

210

of our lives. Fear is useful only when it serves as an alarm clock, a device that wakes us up by briefly ringing but which would drive us crazy if it rang all the time.

When fear takes over, it tends to rob of us creativity, resourcefulness, and freedom. Consider how many students have chosen their subjects not because of a compelling personal interest but because there are likely to be more job opportunities and better pay in this or that field. How many people dare not raise hard and urgent questions with co-workers and bosses because of fear of what might happen were one to speak up? How many choose to have an abortion because of fear of what one's life would be like were the child to be born? How many people fail to tell the truth because of fear? How many people do we fail to meet due to fear?

Many fears are manufactured or hugely inflated by those who find the creation of a climate of dread useful and profitable: fear of refugees, fear of Muslims, fear of terrorists, fear of minorities, fear of the poor, fear of criminals, fear of the police, even fear of our neighbors. Each day we hear reports of tragedies caused by fear, and each day the news gives us a new set of reasons to be afraid. America's craze for guns, even to possess weapons designed for battlefield use, is fear driven. In fact weapons used in war are often fired, with irreversible consequences, because of panic. We now find ourselves in a state of fear-driven permanent war.

The toxic part fear plays in our lives is a point stressed by a prominent Greek Orthodox theologian and bishop, John Zizioulas:

> The essence of sin is the fear of the other, which is part of the rejection of God. Once the affirmation of the "self" is realized through the rejection and not the acceptance of the other . . . it is only natural and inevitable for the other to become an enemy and a threat. . . . The fact that the fear of the other is pathologically inherent in our existence results in the fear not only of the other but of all otherness. This is a delicate point requiring careful consideration, for it shows how deep and widespread fear of the other is: we are not afraid simply of certain others, but even if we accept them, it is on condition that they are somehow like ourselves. Radical otherness is an anathema. Difference itself is a

threat. That this is universal and pathological is to be seen in the fact that even when difference does not in actual fact constitute a threat for us, we reject it simply because we dislike it. Again and again we notice that fear of the other is nothing more than fear of the different. We all want somehow to project into the other the model of our own selves.[2]

What is the antidote for fear? Are there any remedies? How at least can fear play a smaller role in the choices we make? The development of a stronger, deeper spiritual life is surely at the core of an answer. If fear is not to have a dominant role in our lives, a great deal of inner strength is needed. Without it the voice of conscience—and the courage to follow it—will be suppressed.

Behind the popularity of Merton's writing is that he is a door opener and guide to a more contemplative spiritual life. He equips his readers with courage. He also makes it clear that one need nor be a monk to be a contemplative: As he wrote:

The contemplative life has nothing to tell you except to reassure you and say that if you dare to penetrate your own silence and dare to advance without fear into the solitude of your own heart, and risk the sharing of that solitude with the lonely other who seeks God through you and with you, then you will truly recover the light and capacity to understand what is beyond words and beyond explanations because it is too close to be explained: it is the intimate union in the depths of your own heart, of God's spirit and your own secret inmost self, so that you and He are in truth One Spirit.[3]

Yes, the world is scary, but also beautiful, magnificent, mysterious, still undiscovered. How long we live is not as important an issue as how we live.

At the heart of Merton's writing is the message that fear need not rule our lives.

---

2. Extract from "Communion and Otherness"; full text: http://incommunion.org/?p=234.

3. *The Monastic Journey*, ed. Patrick Hart (Kansas City: Sheed Andrews & McMeel, 1977), 173.

Appendix:
Merton's "Marco J. Frisbee" Letter

A satirical letter sent by Thomas Merton (using the pseudonym Marco J. Frisbee) to the editor of Jubilee magazine in February 1962. It was not published at that time and never has been until now.[1]

Dear Sir:

In the recent article [January 1962] on the Rhodes Congress I was struck by the fact that the Russian Orthodox delegates played such an aggressive "peace" role in promoting the Soviet politic of "peace." This of course shows that it is very dangerous for any church to promote a policy of peace, as it will by the very fact cooperate in the insidious work of Red imperialism. I am sure this explains why so many moral theologians in this country are ill at ease with the thought of peace and are putting their best efforts into showing us how nuclear war is the courageous and Christian thing after all. Better dead than red.

At the same time I feel we ought to look for a more original and creative solution to the problem: a solution that will be at once religious and realistic. Frankly I agree with those who are beginning to be weary of the sentimentalism of the Sermon on the Mount.

Of course, I think religion is essential. The spirit of sacrifice is essential too. But don't you agree that the spirit of sacrifice has become effete and subjective in our day? It is a kind of wishy washy moralism, nothing more. And this leads me to my "creative" solution. This solution is realistic, and it calls for intestinal fortitude!

---

1. The text is in the author's Merton archive.

I think we ought to go back to the well-known practice of the Kings of Israel and Judah in the fifth and sixth centuries B.C. when they were having so much trouble with Assyria and Babylon. They too were disgusted by sentimentality and moralism, and they went right-directly into the heart of the problem with a genuine red-blooded, religious rite: *the sacrifice of the first born.*

I fully realize that this suggestion will shock sentimentalists, but this is no time to worry about their cringing susceptibilities. We have got to get sure fire propitiation if we are going to win this war against the irreligious hordes. Here are the advantages of my plan:

1) Morally speaking, it is simply a choice between two evils. We choose the lessor evil. Is junior going to grow up to be a Red Commissar? God forbid. If the war comes junior is going to be dead anyway. If he cooperates in his ritual immolation, he will be doing the greatest thing any man can do. To pass junior through the fire, as the quaint old phrase has it (meaning that junior becomes a whole burnt-offering to Moloch), is only a physical evil, whereas if he has to live under Red domination, that would be a moral evil, we ourselves would sin gravely in exposing him to this danger.

2) There are innumerable secondary gains, or bonuses, connected with this noble act. First of all it will cut down the number of teenagers and make society as a whole more tranquil. I do not of course suggest that you wait until junior becomes a teenager. Better make your offering while he is still under the age of five, when he will be more cooperative and easier to catch.

3) If everybody everywhere can be persuaded to get in on this, it will certainly cut down the danger of the population explosion. But in any case it will mean one less mouth to feed in the family [bomb] shelter.

4) The Kings of Judah sometimes made this offering as part of the consecration of a new fort. You might offer junior to bring down "good luck" on the new shelter.

5) Finally, from the psychological viewpoint, it offers a challenge to the whole rising generation. Junior's brothers and sisters are going to get a new outlook on life from assisting in this moving ceremony.

It will give them an inkling of what it means to live in the modern world, and snap them out of a dangerous dream state induced by any moralistic religious training they may have hitherto received.

I am sure you will take this suggestion in the liturgical spirit in which it is offered.

Yours truly,

Marco J. Frisbee

Books by Thomas Merton
Referred to in This Text

AJ   *The Asian Journal of Thomas Merton*. New York: New Directions, 1973.

AHW   *At Home in the World: The Letters of Thomas Merton and Rosemary Radford Ruether*. Edited by Mary Tardiff. Maryknoll, NY: Orbis Books, 1995.

BTP   *Breakthrough to Peace*. Edited and with an introduction by Thomas Merton. New York: New Directions, 1962.

CF   *Cassian and the Fathers*. Kalamazoo, MI: Cistercian Publications, 2005.

CFT   *The Courage for Truth: Letters to Writers*. Edited by Christine Bochen. New York: Farrar, Straus and Giroux, 1993.

CGB   *Conjectures of a Guilty Bystander*. New York: Doubleday, 1966.

CWL   *Cold War Letters*. Maryknoll, NY: Orbis Books, 2006.

DWL   *Dancing on the Waters of Life: The Journals of Thomas Merton 1963–1965*. Edited by Robert Daggy. San Francisco: HarperSanFrancisco, 1996.

ESF   *Emblems of a Season of Fury*. New York: New Directions, 1963.

FV   *Faith and Violence*. South Bend, IN: University of Notre Dame Press, 1968.

HGL   *The Hidden Ground of Love*. New York: Farrar, Straus and Giroux, 1985.

HR   *"Honorable Reader": Reflections on My Work*. Edited by Robert Daggy. New York: Crossroad, 1986.

MAG   *My Argument with the Gestapo*. New York: Doubleday, 1969.

MJ   *The Monastic Journey*. Edited by Patrick Hart. Kansas City: Sheed Andrews & McMeel, 1977.

NSC   *New Seeds of Contemplation.* New York: New Directions, 1961.

NVA   *The Nonviolent Alternative.* Edited by Gordon Zahn. New York: Farrar, Straus and Giroux, 1980.

OCB   *Original Child Bomb.* New York: New Directions, 1961.

OSM   *The Other Side of the Mountain: The Journals of Thomas Merton 1960–1963.* Edited by Patrick Hart. San Francisco: HarperSanFrancisco, 1996.

PFP   *Passion for Peace.* Edited by William Shannon. New York: Crossroad, 1995.

PPCE   *Peace in the Post-Christian Era.* Maryknoll, NY: Orbis Books, 2004.

RU   *Raids on the Unspeakable.* New York: New Directions, 1964.

RM   *Run to the Mountain: The Journals of Thomas Merton 1939–1941.* Edited by Patrick Hart. San Francisco: HarperSanFrancisco, 1995.

RT   *Redeeming the Time.* London: Burns & Oates, 1966.

SD   *Seeds of Destruction.* New York: Farrar, Straus and Giroux, 1964.

SI   *The Strange Islands.* New York: New Directions, 1957.

SJ   *The Sign of Jonas.* New York: Harcourt, Brace, 1951.

SSM   *The Seven Storey Mountain.* New York: Harcourt, Brace, 1948.

TMLL   *Thomas Merton: A Life in Letters.* Edited by William Shannon and Christine Bochen. New York: HarperOne, 2008.

TTW   *Turning toward the World: The Journals of Thomas Merton 1967–1968.* Edited by Victor Kramer. San Francisco: HarperSanFrancisco, 1998.

WCT   *The Way of Chuang Tzu.* New York: New Directions, 1965.

WD   *Wisdom of the Desert: Some Sayings of the Desert Fathers.* New York: New Directions, 1965.

WTF   *Witness to Freedom: Letters in Times of Crisis.* Edited by William Shannon. New York: Farrar, Straus and Giroux, 1994.

ZBA   *Zen and the Birds of Appetite.* New York: New Directions, 1968.

Index